POINT-
LESS

SARAH M. ZERWIN

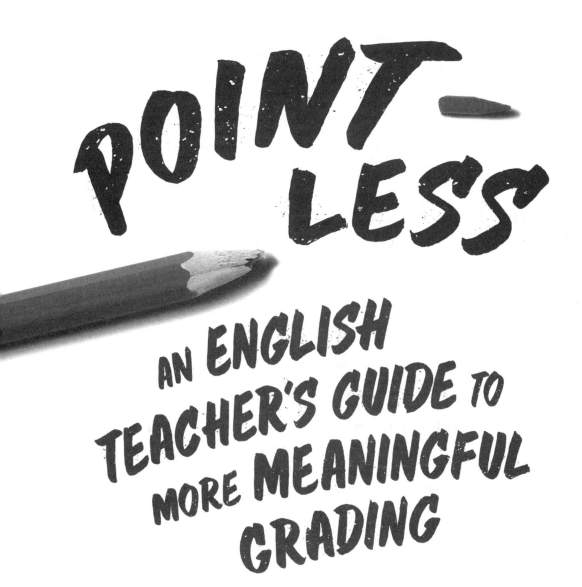

POINT-LESS

AN ENGLISH TEACHER'S GUIDE TO MORE MEANINGFUL GRADING

HEINEMANN
Portsmouth, NH

Heinemann
145 Maplewood Avenue, Suite 300
Portsmouth, NH 03801
www.heinemann.com

Offices and agents throughout the world

The author and publisher wish to thank those who have generously given permission to reprint borrowed material:

> From *In the Best Interest of Students: Staying True to What Works in the ELA Classroom* by Kelly Gallagher, copyright © 2015, reproduced with permission of Stenhouse Publishers. www.stenhouse.com

Acknowledgments for borrowed material continue on page xvi.

Library of Congress Cataloging-in-Publication Data
Name: Zerwin, Sarah M., author.
Title: Point-less : an English teacher's guide to more meaningful grading / Sarah M. Zerwin.
Description: Portsmouth, NH : Heinemann, [2020] | Includes bibliographical references.
Identifiers: LCCN 2019055937 | ISBN 9780325109510
Subjects: LCSH: Grading and marking (Students) | English teachers—In-service training. | Student-centered learning. | Teacher effectiveness.
Classification: LCC LB3051 .Z43 2020 | DDC 371.27/2—dc23
LC record available at https://lccn.loc.gov/2019055937

Editor: Katie Wood Ray
Production: Vicki Kasabian
Text and cover designs: Monica Ann Crigler
Author photograph: Courtney Nicholson-Paine
Typesetter: Shawn Girsberger
Manufacturing: Steve Bernier

Printed in the United States of American on acid-free paper
4 5 RWP 25 24 23 22 21
June 2021 Printing

To Dad

Contents

Online Resources, noted throughout this book, can be found at http://hein.pub/point-less.

Foreword

"Read the world to write your future."

—Sarah Zerwin

DEEP DOWN, WE ALL KNOW THAT POINTS AND LETTER GRADES DON'T really tell us what matters most about students' learning. Teachers want their students to grow over the course of their class, but unfortunately, grading sometimes gets in the way. If you are like me, you're probably tired of spending weekends grading work only to have it thrown in the trash seconds after students discover their grade. You might be frustrated that even when you let students redo assignments, they don't take you up on the offer. Maybe you're wondering how to shift students' focus off of grade grubbing to actual learning. Or, perhaps you're struggling to push students who know how to finesse rubrics and Sparknote books to do more than just play the game of school. You might even be willing to honor growth over mastery if you could just figure out how to manipulate the electronic grade book.

Years ago, I decided that if I were going to spend time grading and writing comments on papers, two things would have to happen. First, I would have to be selfish—and use my assessment time not just to assign points but to get smarter about the needs of students. Second, I would have to slow down and write meaningful feedback each student would immediately apply to their experience of reading and writing. I stumbled again and again trying to make my ideas manageable on a day-to-day basis.

Sarah Zerwin has written the book I desperately needed to help my beliefs about learning match my assessment practices. Inside this book is a treasure trove of new thinking that will guide teachers as they shift students' focus off of points to actual learning. Teachers will find ways to navigate grading obstacles and learn how to repurpose the grade book into a living warehouse of descriptive data that informs feedback and reflection.

Three years ago, I joined a writing group. It was at this retreat that I met Sarah. The first summer I heard the budding ideas for this book. I was very familiar with her building, as my niece and nephews attended it. Sadly, none of them had the privilege of being in her class, but I was pretty sure this new way of grading wasn't going to fly in this community. The second summer, Sarah shared an excerpt from an early draft and I was intrigued. Had she really figured out how to take the focus off of the grade and put it on the learning? Last summer, as she was adding the finishing touches, I was wowed—and I am happy to report that I was wrong! With each chapter, Sarah addresses every grading obstacle one could think of. She provides ways to navigate objections that parents, athletic directors, administrators, colleagues, colleges, and even students might have with this innovative way of reporting grades.

Sarah tempts us to consider that "Learning lives in the process," *not* the final product. She compels us to consider revision as the instructional focus instead of the high-stakes, final product connected to someone else's rubric. Through careful and clear descriptions, Sarah shows teachers how they can make their marking time more effective. Instead of assigning random points to student tasks, she demonstrates how teachers can provide students with concise, descriptive data that serves as meaningful and specific feedback. Sarah's useful way of tracking student growth not only serves students but also helps teachers get feedback as they notice patterns in student learning.

Inside this book, teachers will find:

* online resources rife with tools and examples to manage feedback and student reflections

* powerful examples of student thinking and ways to harness the electronic grade book as a useful instructional tool

* rituals and routines that protect precious time so there are more opportunities for instruction and student revision

* frameworks that hold and guide student and teacher feedback

* strategies that increase students' agency and abilities to read, write, and discuss

* checklists to simplify convoluted rubrics

* provocative questions for teachers and students to ponder and push thinking.

Sarah nudges readers to consider how traditional forms of grading get in the way of student growth. Her pioneering ways of marking, collecting, and sharing student work shows teachers how to assess and evaluate with fidelity in ways that serve student learning. One of my favorite structures in the book are the letters from students who have reflected on their growth as learners. Their words give me courage to consider how to morph the centuries-old grading process into something that honors growth over compliance.

Sarah lives the life of a high school English teacher. She has felt the pain and dread that comes with grading stacks of papers over the weekend. Sarah doesn't just empathize with us, she shows us better ways to manage the grading system so that students get more opportunities to reenter their learning and teachers get more time to teach.

It's exciting to think how reading and writing instruction could change if teachers weren't compelled to evaluate everything students did for the mere purpose of putting points in the grade book. Are you ready to find your path to a better way of grading? Are you ready to lead students on this journey to becoming better readers, writers, and thinkers? If so, you are going to love *Point-Less*!

Cris Tovani
author of *I Read It, but I Don't Get It* and coauthor
of *No More Teaching as Telling*

Acknowledgments

TED ZERWIN, MY DAD, WROTE A BOOK SEVERAL YEARS AGO. IT WAS THE textbook he couldn't find for the graduate courses he was teaching in fundraising and financial management for nonprofit organizations. The book literally spilled out of his head fully formed. I was his (mostly clueless) editor. As I read each chapter and his clear, concise prose recounting his many-year expertise on the topic, I could see him, sitting at his computer and pecking out each page (he typed with index fingers only). I imagined his writing happened absent of fits and starts, the words just flowing from his mind and lining up on the screen in the most orderly fashion possible.

My words don't flow so neatly out of my head. My process involves throwing way too many words at the screen in serpentine sentences, a word vomit you could say, and then struggling to trim them down to something another human can actually follow. My patient editor, Katie Wood Ray, knows better than anyone what I'm talking about. In fact, hidden as a single chapter in the table of contents of an entirely different book I proposed to Katie almost four years ago, she unearthed the topic of this book. I am grateful to her keen ability to see what was there beneath my cascades of words. She carefully helped me to form them into this book. Katie, thank you. Your feedback has made me a better writer and a better teacher of writing. And thank you also to Louisa Irele for her editorial expertise and feedback at a critical time.

Katie never would have even seen my initial book proposal had it not been for the encouragement of Penny Kittle. Thank you, Penny, for attending a presentation by four high school teachers in Colorado all those years ago and challenging us to write.

Heinemann truly is a dream team, comprised of lovely humans I've only just met: Patty Adams, Lauren Audet, Cindy Black, Vicki Boyd, Kim Cahill, Monica Crigler, Sherry Day, Mim Easton, Michelle Flynn, Sarah Fournier, Shawn Girsberger, Michael Grover, Erik Ickes, Vicki Kasabian, Krysten Lebel, Jane Orr, Jillian Sims, Roderick Spelman, Tess Steenbeke, Paul Tomasyan, Brett Whitmarsh. Thank you all for this opportunity, and apologies to those I missed.

Something remarkable happens when you teach alongside the same people for over a decade. Jay Stott and Paul Bursiek started this whole point-less journey years ago when they wondered what would happen if they took the numbers off of the rubric. It was only a matter of time before I would start conducting similar experiments in my own classroom. Jay, office 831 is no more due to the recent renovations to our building, but this book is the outgrowth of the conversations we started in that tiny, cluttered office, with Paul sitting in the third chair. I've done my best to write it all down. Adding on Tracy Brennan, Claire-Maria Broaddus, and Jaime Rodrigues—we've shared office space, classrooms, students, and conference presentations. We've chatted about teaching and life during shared off periods, over lunch, or while walking around the lake in the park next to our school. Thank you for indulging my constant need to reflect and come up with new ways to meet the enduring goals of engaging readers and writers in our classrooms. And for being my dear friends. This book would not be happening without you.

I'm lucky to teach in a department full of great teachers who are wonderful people. They challenge me daily: Chris, Ward, Carla, Jim, Angela, Jim, JohnMichael, Susie, Emily, Courtney, Karen, Aaron, Maura, David, Lanny, Christine, Bri, and (in loving memory of) Steven. I'm grateful to all of you. Thank you also to the rest of my Fairview colleagues and for the school we've built together. I love teaching with you every day.

One of my assistant principals, Sarah Digiacomo, was sitting next to me at a conference presentation the moment I decided I could not do the points thing anymore. She has supported me every step of the way. Neither she nor my principal, Don Stensrud (two more educators I've been lucky to work with for over a decade), has ever told me I couldn't try out something new in my classroom. They—and the entire administration team of my school—trust their teachers as professionals. They support innovation by giving it space and time to grow. Thank you, Don, Sarah, Rose, Ross, T.K., Mike, and Jim.

My three Jedi Masters—Karen Hartman, Tim Hillmer, and Stevie Quate—read and responded to early drafts and have cheered me on from day one. Their presence in my world as teaching and life mentors is invaluable. Thank you for the opportunities with The Colorado Writing Project and for bringing the other teacher consultants into my world: Sheila, Shari, Karen C., Crystal, Amy. It's an honor to sit around the table with you and talk about teaching writing.

There are numerous people in my professional orbit who have talked teaching with me and supported me along this journey. I'm certain I won't be able to collect all of them here, but I'll try. Thank you, Shanie Armbruster, Monica Breed, Jenn Brauner, Tricia Ebarvia, Kate Flowers, Laurel Hauck, Liz Homan, Bonnie Katzive, Allison Marchetti, Christy May, Shaina Maytum, Mitch Nobis, Rebekah O'Dell, Liz Prather, Marilyn Pryle, Diana Rapp, Amy Rasmussen, Karla Scornavacco, Angel Stobaugh, Julia Torres, Jonathan Wright.

Radishes, you know who you are, and you know why. Thank you.

My dissertation adviser at the University of Colorado at Boulder, Bill McGinley, guided me carefully through the adventure of writing my doctoral dissertation over a decade ago, a critical piece of my journey toward this book. Thank you, Bill, and my committee members: Elizabeth Dutro, Margaret Eisenhart, Dan Liston, and Bob Craig. They were all patient readers who challenged my thinking.

Thank you to my brother, John Zerwin. You've always supported me in the things I've taken on in my life, including this book. Like only a brother can, you used to point out that my endless stacks of papers to grade were my own fault for assigning the work. You were right!

Thank you to both my Zerwin and Strode circles for loving me while I worked on this book, even when I had to hole up and write. Mireille, Julia, Mathieu, Scott, (in loving memory of) Joanna, Kyle, Julie, Clare, Susanna, Rob, Laura, Paul. I love you all.

To all my aunties and uncles in Ohio, Michigan, and California and to my cousins across the country, thank you for your love and support.

My mom, Verna Su Zerwin, is perhaps the biggest cheerleader I have in my life. Thank you, Mom, for your unending belief in what I'm capable of. The day I told you this book was going to happen, you said you knew Dad was jumping up and down in heaven about the news. If only I could have a fraction of the impact on people that he had in his life.

Where do I start with my husband, Paul Strode, and our daughter, Jane? You put up with me during the day-to-day while I managed this project on top of a full-time teaching job. Thank you. You supported me with a backyard shed writing escape, with long walks, with good food, with games of Wingspan, and with episodes of *Gilmore Girls*, *Queer Eye*, and *Stranger Things* and by keeping the household humming along while I hid away to write, by talking with me through different aspects of this book over dinners out, by going on road trips and camping trips to give me time to write, by sending Daisy Dog out to the shed to keep me company, and by umpteen other things that you do. I love you both dearly. Thank you for sharing this life with me.

Thank you to the students who graciously allowed me to use their work in this book so that my readers may see what has kept me moving along this point-less journey.

And finally, to my students, past, present, and future. You are my reason for all of this. You rock, and you deserve a classroom that inspires you to read and write. You are so much more than point collectors. Thank you for letting me be your teacher.

Introduction

Dear Reader,

The "Sacred Box of Writing" filled up from class period to class period until it was overflowing. I watched it, the foreboding building in me as I anticipated the time I would have to spend to make my way through it. Maybe it was a Friday. I would pack up the papers in the box and stuff them into folders and then into my bag to lug home for the weekend, promising myself that I would dive into them first thing Saturday morning so I could bask in the rest of the weekend unencumbered. The bag would sit there all weekend, taunting me, reminding me, calling to me, placing a pallor over my Friday evening, my Saturday, my Sunday morning, and completely ruining my Sunday evening. And Monday morning, defeated, I would drag the bag back to school with most of the papers ungraded.

Grading was by far the worst part of my job. One thing I mean by "grading" is when I sat down with a rubric and a stack of papers (or stared down a list of documents on my computer screen), knowing I had hours of work to do. The other thing I mean by "grading" is the expectation that teachers must collect and evaluate everything students do, affixing some kind of numerical measure to each piece of student work so that the grade book can math everything into a constantly updating, constantly broadcasted, high-stakes grade.

I found that if I thought differently about the second thing I meant by grading, it helped me with the first. Maybe I didn't need to collect and evaluate everything my students did. Maybe I didn't need to put numbers and points on everything (or anything?).

I simply started by not putting points on things anymore. And my students still did the work. And their parents didn't yell at me. And students still learned and grew—perhaps more than they had before. Everything turned out OK.

I'm writing this to you after my eleventh semester without points. I've definitely made plenty of mistakes along the way, and I'm still figuring things out. I'm no assessment expert. I'm a high school teacher who just couldn't spend any more time evaluating student work with points and grades, and I'm working to find a different approach.

By the time you're reading this, I'm sure that what I'm doing in my classroom has evolved. But the core is here. I will continue to focus on the learning that matters, build my classroom on that, share the feedback load with my students, use my grade book to reveal learning without points, ask students to choose their own direction for their learning and track their own progress, and make the instances my school requires grades an opportunity for students to self-reflect and decide for themselves what their grades should be.

This book starts with an argument for thinking about grading differently, and then it moves through a process to refocus a classroom on readers and writers and their learning. As you read, remember that you know your teaching context better than anyone else, and you'll almost certainly need to tweak this process and adapt it to meet the needs of your students.

In between each chapter I've included examples of semester grade letters from my students and from students of my colleagues. These letters will help you imagine what it might look like to get to final grades without points. I've also tried to address the obstacles that may pop up in your thinking with some "Navigating Obstacles" thought bubbles along the way. My hope is that these will help you move from thinking "That would never work for my school" to looking for the ways things actually *could* work. Where are the nooks where you can start to push back at the expected grading system?

I never thought I could run my classroom without points. Not for where I teach. Not for the students I teach. But I was wrong, and so much more is possible than I ever imagined.

With gratitude,
Sarah M. Zerwin

Chapter One

Acknowledge the Problems with Points

"DEAR DOC Z," LEO'S LETTER BEGAN. "THROUGH MY HARD WORK AND my growth as a learner during this semester, I believe that an A best reflects my work."

In the letter I ask each of my students to write at the end of the semester, Leo went on to explain how he had grown in my class as a reader, a writer, and a risk-taker and why he thought he should receive an A for his work. In this excerpt from the letter, he reflects specifically on his growth as a writer:

This semester I was able to work very hard and revise two pieces of writing extensively. The first piece of writing that I revised was my narrative story about making a save while I was lifeguarding at a lake in Wisconsin last summer. After you, Cole, Eddie, and Brian left comments, I knew that I had a good piece of writing on my hands. Instead of leaving a good piece a good piece, I decided to revise it to make it even better. After I revised it, I was able to meet with you one on one, to receive more help and suggestions on things that could improve. I was able to turn a good piece into a great one. In your own words "you totally reworked this—new hook even. You fixed errors and had to cut the word count down to under 650."

The second piece that I was able to revise extensively was my feature. When I first turned it in you could barely call it a piece of writing. It was merely a few different paragraphs that barely connected. I was able to do a ton of research and form a much better piece. After that it was brought to my attention that my piece was more like a research paper rather than a feature. I was then able to add things like anecdotes at the start of my piece and subtitles.

Leo's letter is the culmination of an ongoing conversation I had with him about his work and his learning over the course of the entire semester. Along the way, we collected rich data to document his progress, and when I reflected on that information, I agreed with Leo. I thought an A was the best reflection of his work.

I haven't always gotten to grades this way in my teaching, and the conversations I used to have with students about their grades were very different. For example, several years ago, one of my juniors—let's call him Jack—ended up with an 89.4 percent in my class at the end of second semester. He asked me to round up his grade.

I explained that if he had chosen to complete the optional rewrites on his papers, he could have earned more points and the conversation we were having would be unnecessary. I thought that was the end of it.

But then he emailed me, asking me again to round his grade to an A. And then his dad emailed me, followed by his mom, and then Jack yet again. Next, his dad called me on the phone, and there were several more emails. In each instance, I explained that Jack did not complete the optional rewrites.

It seemed to me that in their persistence, Jack and his parents didn't care that it would be unfair to other students who had similar grades for me to round up his and not theirs. They didn't care that it was actually language arts department policy not to round grades. They didn't care that Jack had chosen not to continue working on his writing when given the option, something that would have made him a better writer and brought his grade up along the way. All they cared about was what an A would mean on Jack's transcript when he applied to college the following year.

Finally, at an end-of-year teacher appreciation breakfast, Jack's dad walked into the cafeteria just as I had made my way through the buffet line.

He was looking for me.

"It can't hurt to ask you just one more time," he said.

I held my plate of food in one hand, my cup of juice in the other, and my composure as well as I could. His presence felt invasive, inappropriate, and way too aggressive. All I wanted was to sit with my colleagues and celebrate the end of the school year. I wondered how he even got past the front office, or who told him where all the teachers were, or how he had the gumption to walk into this celebration to ask me one more time to round up his son's grade. But I stood my ground, and off he went.

These two stories about students and their grades couldn't be more different, and this book is about the journey that led me from Jack to Leo—a journey to reconsider grading practices that get in the way of student learning.

I teach in a large, comprehensive, traditional American public high school where grades matter, and getting to grades via points and percentages is the seemingly unquestioned norm. I am required to use an electronic grade book that asks for points to convert into percentages that translate into grades. In the past, I would use my syllabus to detail how students could earn or lose points, and I would review those guidelines at back-to-school night with their parents. At parent–teacher conferences, I explained to parents where students lost points and what they (the students) could do to improve their overall percentage.

Jack's story came to be in my points-driven, do-the-work-or-there-will-be-a-grade-penalty classroom that focused on grades instead of learning. This grading system was what we lived in my school, it is what we had always done, and there seemed no other way to go about it. When a couple of my colleagues down the hall began playing around with different ways to get to grades, I fought them. Vociferously. I just could not see my way around the obstacles in my head.

Yet, little things were biting at my thinking. I invited students to revise to earn higher grades on papers, but the process didn't produce actual revision. The few who took me up on the offer would simply examine the rubric and determine the easiest path to earning a few more points. How could I get all of my students to engage in actual revision? And how could I get them writing more frequently? I was able to grade maybe three process papers per semester at most, and that was not nearly enough writing for my students to really grow as writers. I also wondered how I could get my students to read more books, not just to collect points, but because reading matters.

Questions like these were in my head at the 2013 National Council of Teachers of English Annual Convention when I heard Alfie Kohn speak and lay out an argument against grades. Kohn helped me to see that until I found a way to create a classroom that didn't orbit around grades, my students would focus on collecting points to cash in for grades instead of on the critical learning they need to do as readers and writers. The first step to finding this classroom was to clearly articulate the problems with grading so I could confront them. To move somewhere new, I needed to understand what I was leaving behind and why.

Points-Based Grading Gets in the Way of Student Learning

The firmly entrenched approach to grading in most U.S. high schools operates on a familiar exchange: student compliance for points and grades. This grading system dictates far more than simply how we keep track of our students' work. The exchange (Willis 1977) is how we entice students to do the tasks we ask of them, how we hold them accountable, and how we report out their progress. The ways students can earn and lose points organize what we do in class with them every day. The grade becomes central. All eyes—students', teachers', parents'—may focus on grades above all else.

Like most teachers, I didn't just decide one day that I would be the manager of the points—this role is wrapped up in the job, emphasized everywhere. The grade book I'm required to use asks for points. My district has a policy about what percentage of my students' grades must draw on data that reflect their learning rather than other factors such as effort or completion. This suggests I'm supposed to math my way to grades.

So, for most of my career, I dangled points in front of my students to keep them working. They would ask incessantly, "How many points is this?" They would ask for extra credit opportunities to bring in extra points. They would negotiate with me for an extra point here or there. I would spell out how I would award points for every task and threaten to take off points for late work or for students not being focused in class. Talk about points took up so much airtime that I became convinced my students would not do anything unless they knew points were at stake.

Though I also talked about how reading and writing was the most important work students would do for themselves in school, the emphasis on points betrayed that message. The points gave *me* power rather than helping my students see the power they had themselves as readers and writers.

The encounter with Jack hinged on what he and his parents thought he should get in exchange for the work that he did. They wanted the grade with the highest value, regardless of whether or not Jack's work warranted it. Even more, their constant requests to round up the grade suggested they felt he was entitled to the grade no matter what.

"Students begin to view academic wealth as determined by the number of points they can accumulate" (Guskey and Bailey 2001, 19), and in the context where I teach, parents and students see academic wealth as real and consequential. Over 90 percent of the seniors in my high school go on to college—they can literally cash in their grades for college admissions. Hence, the points-based system at the center of my classroom encouraged many of my students to focus on point collecting instead of learning—even though I thought I had designed their assignments so they would collect points while doing meaningful work.

I also had students who, for a wide variety of reasons, frequently ended up with low grades. Maybe the tricks of point collecting were a mystery to them, or maybe what they could get in the grades-for-compliance exchange wasn't terribly meaningful, or maybe the heavy focus on points obscured their view of why reading and writing are critical to their lives as human beings. Whatever the case, my classroom's focus on points hurt these students.

As for my students who valued high grades, they often took shortcuts to get the points without doing much learning. I could see what they were doing because it's what I did myself in high school. I wanted my straight As, and it was possible to collect the points necessary to get there without working terribly hard at reading or writing. Reading summaries and commentaries instead of the books I was assigned worked well enough. Writing papers at the very last minute also worked well enough. I had no reason to work harder when the shortcuts I took got me where I wanted to be: graduating high school with a grade point average over 4.0.

In over two decades, my teaching career has taken me from urban to suburban to semirural settings to my current teaching life in a college town. In each setting, I have had students who buy in to the grades-for-compliance exchange and all it will enable them to get in their lives, and I've had students who don't buy in, who squeak by (or don't) with the grades they need to pass the class so they can just leave high school behind. But in either case, because I was focused only on points, I wasn't able to invite all of my students into the work of authentic reading and writing.

In the following sections, I'd like to consider four specific ways a points-based approach to grading, what I'll refer to as "the grading system," subverts our efforts to inspire students to be readers and writers in a complex world.

The Grading System Rewards Compliance over Learning

I believe my students want to learn. They want to spend their hours in school doing meaningful work. They want to be challenged. They want to leave school each day with knowledge that will help them to achieve their dreams and goals and prepare them for success in their future. I believe this is true even for the most resistant students.

The rewards and punishments of a points-based grading system, however, often supersede students' natural interest in learning. Students may have a desire to get better grades, but that desire gets in the way of their authentic engagement. Compliantly, they "chase marks and become less interested in the learning itself" (Kohn 2011). They read because there will be a test that impacts their final grade. They write because if they don't, they'll lose points. They don't read or write to explore their own ideas, and research speaks to the impact of this on student learning. According to Kohn, research shows that:

1. Grading tends to diminish students' interest in whatever they're learning.

2. Grading creates a preference for the easiest possible task.

3. Grading tends to reduce the quality of students' thinking.

Kohn explains that the research shows that *all* grades lead to these predictable effects—grades based on points, grades that emphasize compliance, standards-based grades, grades alongside narrative assessments of students' work—anything that attempts to reduce student learning to a number or a letter for the purpose of rating and ranking students. He argues that we must work toward eliminating grades entirely, and along the way, minimize the impact of any grades we can't avoid.

A grading system based on compliance is especially damaging for students who simply won't work for grades and points. The extrinsic motivation means nothing to them. They may or may not show up to class. When they are there, they may do little, no matter how serious the consequences for their grade. They need a totally different invitation to engage in the work of school, an invitation that has nothing to do with grades. But stuck in the grading system, these students are left with no real reason to work in school and do not even begin to practice the reading and writing skills they need to be full agents of their own lives.

As others before me have said, the grading system is assessment done *to* students rather than assessment done *with* them as equal partners in their learning, and there is a constant threat of grade and point penalties when students don't comply with what we ask of them. The system forces students to work and monitors them constantly, broadcasting their compliance or noncompliance out via the electronic grade book at every moment. Students learn from the system that what they do in school is not for their own benefit, but rather to satisfy whoever monitors their work—teachers, parents, school administrators, college admissions counselors, and on and on.

The Grading System Asks Us to Measure the Immeasurable

No series of numbers can adequately capture a student's meaningful, authentic work as a reader and writer, and yet the grading system asks us to quantify the quality of a thesis statement, or the strength of a student's response to something they've read, or how well a piece of writing does in each of the categories on a rubric. Kohn (2011) explains, "Once we're compelled to focus only on what can be reduced to numbers, such as how many grammatical errors are present in a composition . . . , thinking has been severely compromised. And that is exactly what happens when we try to fit learning into a four- or five- or (heaven help us) 100-point scale."

The problem is, of course, that the most important reading and writing work our students need to do is not quantifiable. We need them to develop lives as readers. We need them to work with words to capture their thoughts and questions about the world and to communicate them in ways that move readers. This work takes time, risks, reflection, mistakes, starting over, sticking with it. We can describe what all of this looks like, but measuring it fails to capture its full complexity.

Epiphanies, for example, are an indication of growth for readers and writers. Imagine a student finally realizes why it's important to read books in our smartphone world, and he begins reading for his own purposes as a human being. This is a serious win. It matters. It's *the* work we want for our students. How do we measure that? Is that a 10-point epiphany? Or just a 7-point epiphany because it took the student a few weeks to get there? As soon as we quantify learning like this, it becomes just another number and not a critically important moment in the student's journey as a reader.

Instead of traditional points and percentages, grades based on standards typically use "levels of proficiency that illustrate a natural progression of quality" (Schimmer 2016, 49). Proficiency levels make learning data comparable across students and can help us to determine if they need more support, but whether the levels are numbered (usually 1–4 or 1–5) or identified with descriptive labels such as *emerging, partially proficient, proficient, advanced*, and so on, the same problems persist. As Kohn suggests, our thinking about student learning is compromised when we try to fit it into any kind of scale, and proficiency levels are a predetermined scale.

Without question, quantification and measurement prioritize ranking and sorting—the difference between 89.4 percent and 90 percent is very consequential—over cultivating learning—"I was able to do a ton of research and form a much better piece."

The Grading System Suggests Objectivity, but It Is Not Objective

When it comes to data, it's easy to think that numbers are more objective than words, and the grading system expects us to fill our grade books with numbers that reflect student learning. Even though we are dealing with the immeasurable, we must devise some way to arrive at numbers, so we create rubrics that define how students can earn or lose points on a task. But be honest. How consistently can a teacher *objectively* follow a rubric from paper to paper? We are not always perfect evaluation machines—teachers are human after all. What if the teacher is tired? Or impatient? Or not thinking clearly? Is it possible to award or take off more points depending on the time of day or how rested the teacher is?

According to Guskey and Bailey (2001), "Grades have long been recognized in the measurement community as prime examples of unreliable measurement" (12). And the more analytical the grading approach (i.e., with multiple categories on a rubric, each with a unique score), the more opportunities for variability to enter into grading (32). In our efforts to make grading as objective as possible with clear and detailed rubrics, we actually make the process *more* subjective.

For all their illusive objectivity, the numbers we record in points-based grade books create other issues as well. For example, there is an ongoing debate (Wormeli 2006) about the 0 and the inordinate effect it has on a student's grade. Some say you should put in 50 instead of 0 to indicate a missed assignment. Other teachers bristle at that because it seems to give students credit for doing nothing. This debate never considers that the problem might be with the grading system itself that requires us to use numbers to document student learning.

All the options we have when we set up our grade books can also trouble with objectivity. What difference will checking the box to weight categories make in students' grades? How many points should each assignment be worth? What happens if we change grade book settings after there are already several grades recorded—are the resulting changes to students' grades fair?

The bottom line is, when every single set of points collected goes into a grade book and calculates into an overall, high-stakes grade, our human variances and inconsistencies belie objectivity and can have real consequences for our students. On the other hand, our professional, individualized assessments of our students' work based on what we know about them as learners can render detailed and accurate descriptions of their learning (Guskey and Bailey 2001, 33). Words may be more subjective, but they are also powerful data. Just consider how much more you know about what Leo learned in my class from just two paragraphs of written data than you do from knowing that Jack's grade was an 89.4 percent.

The Grading System Doesn't Provide the Information We Need

Leo's letter about his learning reveals so much that he can use to move forward in his work as a writer. The role that feedback played in his development, for example, is clear, and it's something he should seek out with future pieces of writing. Contrast that insight to what you might glean from typical points-based grade book data like that captured in Figure 1.1.

What does this tell us about the student as a writer? There's an upward trend in the scores (except for the third one), but why? And what happened on that third paper? The numbers don't provide this information. And what did the student write about for each paper? Which did she choose to revise? What risks did she take? What did the growth look like across these five tasks specifically—was there stronger

Assignment	Points possible	Points earned	Score
Song/video analysis argument draft	20	16	80.0
Advertisement analysis argument draft	20	17	85.0
Satire analysis argument draft	20	12	60.0
A Place to Stand analysis argument draft	20	18	90.0
Revision of an analysis argument	50	47	94.0
OVERALL GRADE	**130**	**110**	**84.6**

Figure 1.1 Typical points-based grade book data

use of language? Was there more detailed support? Was the content more complex? Were there fewer errors? There is little here that helps us understand this student's journey in a way that will lead to more effective teaching.

Now imagine a student looking at this same collection of points. How well does it invite her to think about what she's learned or how she's grown? She sees only points that calculate into an overall grade that may have serious, concrete consequences for her. She's wondering why she lost points on those earlier tasks. She sees an upward trend and produced writing that falls into the A category, but she still has a B because of the points collected on earlier papers. Will she ever be able to bring that grade up? How many points does she need to earn on the next paper to jump into the A category? Rather than thinking about how the writing she's done has helped her to grow, all she's thinking about is what she can do to earn more points to make that grade go up.

Students *should* be the single most important users of classroom data about their learning. They should know for themselves what they know, what they need to learn, and how they are progressing. Trapped in the grading system, however, they sit and wait for the numbers in the grade book to tell them all this—and the numbers reveal very little that's useful. I realize it is possible that Jack really thought that a B didn't accurately reflect what he learned in my class. I was still standing firmly in the traditional grading system, however, so all we had to talk about was how the numbers in the grade book resulted in an 89.4 percent. What he knew about his own experience just didn't factor in to the conversation about his semester grade.

How Did We Get Here?

If the grading system is so problematic, you may be wondering, how did it become so firmly entrenched as a system in schools? That's a good question, and like so many stories in history, it's complicated by who has power and who doesn't.

The obsession with measuring student learning goes back to America of the late 1800s and early 1900s, when there was a massive influx of immigrants from Eastern and Southern Europe. In fact, this period birthed the American high school as we know it, designed via high technology of the day, the factory model. New high schools were opening at the rate of one per week (Tyack 1974), and the factory model made it possible for teachers to take on greater numbers of students. To manage these larger caseloads, high school teachers began using percentages and grades to report out student learning (Guskey and Bailey 2001, 25).

The field of educational measurement began about the same time, but it wasn't focused solely on learning. Psychologists developed "mental engineering" based on mental testing to provide justification for ranking and sorting humans to maintain social hierarchies (Wilson 2018, 33). Some felt threatened by the new immigrants, and they used science to justify their efforts to keep them in a certain place: "Scales join an entire battery of practices (including eugenics) purposely created to enforce racial, ethnic, and economic hierarchies. Educational measurement didn't just incidentally support these efforts: the field emerged to substantiate them. Its tools (scales, rubrics, calibration) are methods of oppression" (32).

Yes, oppression.

Asao B. Inoue (2015) illustrates this continuing oppression in his book, *Antiracist Writing Assessment Ecologies*. He unpacks how the scales we use to evaluate writing swim in a white racial frame that fails to see clearly the learning of many nonwhite students. Yet we still rely on such scales to measure student learning, as if it is an objective quantity that increases neatly in the same way for every human. Grade scales. ACT scores. SAT scores. International Baccalaureate test scores. Advanced Placement test scores. Reading intervention scores. (I could go on.) We can trace these scales back to early efforts to measure intelligence, even "an outgrowth of the science of skull measurement," that sought to correlate skull size with intelligence (Wilson 2018, 34–35). This research was long ago debunked of course, but we cannot divorce the scales we use now from their more insidious origins.

We continue to use scales to rank and sort humans, and in school, every scale we use to measure our students' learning suggests to them that they are better than the students who rank lower on the scale and not as good as the students who rank higher. And because it all appears objective and scientific, they take it as some kind of statement of their worth. The grading system has a long history of keeping students in their place, but it doesn't have to be that way.

Navigating Obstacles 1.1

I'm worried my district would never let me move away from traditional grading.

If you have this worry, try to find pockets of support. Make connections and build trust as you advocate for what's best for your students as learners. Even if you don't all agree, your colleagues can be powerful partners in this work.

I'm lucky to work with smart colleagues and administrators who have helped me on my journey to rethink my grading practices. But it has been a journey of years. And we're still on it. Some of the things we've tried along the way haven't worked out very well, but we try to build on the ones that seem to fire up our students a bit more, get our classrooms humming along more productively, and provide space for students to do work that matters to them.

Finally, be sure to look closely at what your district actually does ask of you. You may be surprised by what you find. The teacher evaluation standards in my district ask us to create classrooms where students assume ownership for evaluating and monitoring their own progress, so the work I'm doing against the grading system is in fact the exact work that my district wants me to take on, even if it seems to go against how many teachers approach grading.

We Can Choose a Different Path to Grades

In his luncheon address at the Conference for English Leadership in November of 2017, Cornelius Minor said, "To be neutral in a moving stream is to go with the current." Systems are like machines, he explained, and machines keep running without their operators unless we actively turn them off. I believe that the route to grades through points for compliance is a system that we need to actively switch off.

The grading system sets our students up to do whatever it takes to earn the points they need for the grades they want. This is why they cram for tests and forget everything the next day, take every shortcut they can find, pretend to read, and write just to complete assignments. This is why they sometimes justify cheating. But students don't control the system that causes all this. The people with power in schools do.

The grading system is heavily entrenched, and it may seem difficult to move, but as Maja Wilson reminds us, "we don't need to wait for the entire system to change to work toward assessment that supports growth. . . . There are gaps in the system—small, hidden spaces in which to evade, ignore, resist, and reframe assessment mandates" (2018, 131).

Finding these gaps is challenging, I know, and risky. The grading system seems too pervasive, too expected of us, too embedded in the required grade books and official records that come out of our classrooms. It seems risky to go against what most of our colleagues are doing. We worry about our classrooms. Will everything fall apart if we remove the center that students have become accustomed to? What if they stop doing anything at all without the usual reward of points for grades?

And the truth is, of course, most of us cannot just refuse to provide the semester grades that students need for their official transcripts. This wouldn't work in my school community for reasons that are bigger than my realm of influence as a classroom teacher. Even so, we can work to build classrooms that lower our students' academic stress and free them up to take risks to learn and grow as readers and writers. We can help them develop reading practices they can sustain for their entire lives. We can invite them to struggle with the process of writing as they seek just the right way to formulate their words to communicate what they want to say to a particular audience for a particular purpose. We just need a different path to get to grades, and this book is about finding that path.

The chapters that follow move along one possible path, the one I've followed on my journey to shift my students' attention away from points and onto learning. Each step along the way is based on a critical realization that helped me understand how I could get to grades in a different way.

The first realization is that we can't teach everything expected of us and still do the kind of in-depth, descriptive assessment that inspires readers and writers. We often turn to the efficiency of grades to manage achievement data on dozens of required curriculum standards, but why not choose what we teach more intentionally, with a narrower focus and more targeted, descriptive assessment? In Chapter 2, I'll show you how to establish clear and meaningful learning goals to sit at the center of instruction and assessment in your classroom.

The second realization is that we teach students, not content, but yet we build our classrooms around products to be graded—research papers, exams, presentations, and so on. What if we thought of our students and the readers and writers they need to become as the product instead? In Chapter 3, I'll show you how to carefully plan what happens in your classroom so that students and grades are focused on the work itself—the messiness of reading and writing—rather than on completing products for points.

The third realization is that students need to write far more than we are able to respond to on our own. Typically, we toil alone for hours over stacks of student papers. But the teacher is not the only person in the room who can manage the feedback load. In Chapter 4, I'll show you how to build a community focused on feedback where you share the load of response with students so they get the experience they need to grow as readers and writers.

The fourth realization is a lucky one. If you are required to use an electronic grade book, it may seem like you have to enter only quantifiable data, but you don't. In Chapter 5, I will show you how I learned to hack my required grade book and turn it into a source of rich, qualitative data students can use to evaluate their own learning.

Chapter 6 is based on the realization that most students will own their work more if they have some say in determining what that work will be. In this chapter I'll show you how to teach students to set individual learning goals and reflect on their progress consistently.

We don't *have* to leave it up to the math machine in the grade book to determine students' final grades. Instead, we can use the final grade (and any required progress grades along the way) as an opportunity for inspiring conversations with students about their learning growth. In Chapter 7 I'll show you how to organize to have these conversations and then make decisions about final grades.

Finally, I know how impossible it may seem to stop grading with points. In the Afterword, I hope to inspire you to get started with a few simple places to begin.

RESOURCES TO HELP YOU ON YOUR JOURNEY

Many educators are actively taking on the grading system. Their work has inspired my own thinking, as you'll see throughout this book. Here's an annotated list of resources I've found helpful along the way.

✶ Bower, Joe, and Paul Thomas, eds. 2013. *De-Testing + De-Grading Schools: Authentic Alternatives to Accountability and Standardization.* New York: Peter Lang.

This book is a collection of articles about testing and grading pulled together by two smart educators. Sadly, Joe Bower has passed away, but his blog, *For the Love of Learning*, is still accessible (www.joe-bower.blogspot.com/). Paul Thomas blogs frequently at *Radical Eyes for Equity* (www.radicalscholarship .wordpress.com).

✶ Guskey, Thomas, and Jane Bailey. 2001. *Developing Grading and Reporting Systems for Student Learning.* Thousand Oaks, CA: Corwin Press.

Often when people find out what I'm writing about, they say something about Guskey. He's done prolific research on grading. I found this particular book with Jane Bailey most useful. He has a 2015 book, *On Your Mark: Challenging the Conventions of Grading and Reporting.* It's good, but the Guskey and Bailey book covers the same ground and more.

✶ Inoue, Asao B. 2015. *Antiracist Writing Assessment Ecologies: Teaching and Assessing Writing for a Socially Just Future.* Fort Collins, CO: WAC Clearinghouse and Anderson, SC: Parlor Press.

Inoue's book provides a deep dive into how the traditional approach to writing assessment expected by the grading system perpetuates a white racial valuing of language and expression. He teaches composition at the college level, but his labor-based contract grading is powerful and adaptable to middle and high school classrooms. I love his emphasis on the *doing* of the work for the grade.

✻ Kohn, Alfie. 2011. "The Case Against Grades." www.alfiekohn.org/article/case
-grades.
This short essay is seminal in the world of resisting traditional grading. If you
read nothing else, read this.

✻ *Teachers Going Gradeless* (blog). www.teachersgoinggradeless.com.
This online community (find them on Facebook, too) is an excellent place
for support, resources, and connecting with like-minded educators. Cocre-
ator Arthur Chiaravalli's post, "Teachers Going Gradeless: Toward a Future of
Growth Not Grades" (April 8, 2017) is a great place to start to get a sense of
what the group is all about.

✻ Torres, Julia. 2018. "Going Gradeless in Urban Ed." *Teachers Going Gradeless*.
www.teachersgoinggradeless.com/blog/2018/03/10/urban-ed.
In this post, Julia Torres takes on grading issues in urban education in
thoughtful detail.

✻ Wilson, Maja. 2006. *Rethinking Rubrics in Writing Assessment*. Portsmouth,
NH: Heinemann.
I used to be a complete rubric devotee, even when my quest for developing
the perfect rubric left me constantly disappointed. This book helped me to
understand why.

✻ Wilson, Maja. 2018. *Reimagining Writing Assessment: From Scales to Stories*.
Portsmouth, NH: Heinemann.
Seldom do I need at least a week to ponder each chapter before moving
on—but I did with this book. Wilson shows how the scales we use to assess
students are detrimental and offers a powerful alternative for assessment:
story.

Interlude

Semester Grade Letter by Izzy, Grade 12, AP English Literature and Composition

Dear Doc Z,

When I was younger my family and teachers used to boast about how good of a writer and reader I was. From a young age literature fascinated me, and throughout my elementary school years I constantly was reading, whether it was *Captain Underpants* or *The Diary of Anne Frank*. In my writing classes, I was an eager learner. I wrote poetry and stories, always using my writing as a creative outlet. I was proud of what I could do with a pencil in my hand.

In this excerpt from Izzy's letter, she articulates what seems to be a common trajectory in students' learning journeys. I, too, loved reading and writing in elementary school, but didn't so much by the time I got to high school. I've found that moving away from points invites students like Izzy to reconnect with what they loved about reading and writing when they were younger.

When I took the step from elementary school to middle school, it seemed that reading and writing suddenly became "lame." I still loved language arts, and I still excelled in those classes, but pressure from my peers made me more hesitant to outwardly share and enjoy my love of literature. I didn't talk about the books that I was reading with my friends anymore, and I never wrote stories unless I was assigned to.

By the time that I finally graduated from middle school, I was ready to take a real language arts class, and focus on my favorite subject again. I thought I would once again be surrounded by students who were eager and willing to read and write, just like me.

Spoiler alert: high school students don't like to read and write, and the books and papers that they are forced to finish don't interest them. This hard truth hit me straight in the face as I entered high school as a timid Freshman. Uninterested by the books that I was assigned to read, I quickly learned how to cut corners in my Language Arts classes. I learned how to Spark Note, how to Shmoop, and how to write a mindless five-paragraph academic essay. I continued to succeed in English, always earning As in my supposedly "advanced" classes, but I never truly felt like I was getting much out of what I was learning. I was bored and uninterested. I never cheated, I always showed up to class, and I got straight As, but I felt like I needed more.

That takes me to the beginning of my senior year of high school. Sitting in my second period LA class on the first day of school, you told me that I was going to be able to argue for my grade, and that I was going to set my own learning goals. Still in the mindset that I had adopted from previous years of high school language arts classes, I was thrilled to hear this news. No grades and independent learning sounded awesome to me, because it seemed like less work.

I quickly realized that that was not the case. I figured out that I was going to be held accountable for my own learning, and that I was finally getting the opportunity that I had always wanted to again explore my creativity and push myself in an English class. I began to change my mindset, and soon instead of preparing to cut corners, I was preparing to enjoy reading and writing again.

In the first month of school, I received the task of creating my own learning goals, which was something that I had never done before. I came up with three learning goals: to learn to revise my papers until they are near perfect, to read ALL of the books I am assigned plus more individually, and finally to use my writer's notebook as a creative extension of my mind. I wrote those goals down, making them real, and began my journey to achieving them. . . .

Chapter 6 focuses on students choosing learning goals and tracking their growth toward them.

As I write the story of my growth this semester, I can't help but be shocked by how much this semester has changed my mindset and work ethic in LA. I am being completely honest when I say that I have once again found my passion for reading and writing. I am excited to read and write again, and I no longer feel the pressure to pretend that that is not the case. I feel like I can be creative in this class, which gives me the freedom to express myself through the work that I do. I have achieved all of my goals and grown as a learner this year. I have fallen in love with reading and writing again, and I think that that has shown through the work that I have put into this class. I believe that an A would be an accurate representation of my growth this semester, because I truly have not only done what this class required, but I have taken what I was provided by you and used it to further understand literature and the world.

I agreed with Izzy's selection of an A. Chapter 7 shows the guidelines I give my students to help them select a grade at semester's end.

Sincerely,
Izzy

Chapter Two

Establish Clear and Meaningful Learning Goals

ONE THING IS FOR CERTAIN ABOUT THE PATH TO A GRADE IN A points-based system—it's clear and tidy. Students know exactly what tasks they will be doing, how points are earned and lost, and how many points each task is worth. Collected points calculate into an overall grade determined by a percentage-based scale.

A TYPICAL GRADING OVERVIEW FROM A SYLLABUS

Major assignments (80 percent of overall grade):

- Eight weekly drafts, 20 points each
- Three revised pieces, 50 points each
- Major semester piece of writing, 100 points
- Final exam, 100 points

Minor assignments (20 percent of overall grade):

- Reading quizzes, 10 points each
- Writer's notebook checks, 10 points each
- Group tasks, 10 points each
- Independent reading check-in, 10 points each

Grade penalties:

- Late work: 10 percent deduction per day late
- Not following MLA format: 10 percent deduction
- Cheating/plagiarism: 0 (first offense); failing the class (second offense)

Grade scale:

▸ 90–100% = A
▸ 80–89% = B
▸ 70–79% = C
▸ 60–69% = D
▸ below 60% = F

A points-based grading system is an anchor; its very design eliminates ambiguity. The first semester I tried to move away from points-based grading and focus my students on their learning, I found myself adrift fairly quickly when it came time to decide on final grades. I still had to give them, and I was without my anchor. I knew it as soon as Thomas (pseudonym) and I started our conversation.

"An A."

This was his response to my question about what grade he thought he had earned for the semester. It was May of 2014. Thomas was in my senior class, and graduation was just a few weeks away. He was sitting in the extra chair next to my desk for his grade conference.

My gut told me he hadn't earned that A.

An awkward silence descended.

My first few grade conferences had been lovely because the students and I pretty much agreed on the semester grade as if there was some magical, shared, internalized knowledge about what As, Bs, and Cs look like.

Thomas twiddled the pencil he had in his hand. My eyes searched my desk for something, anything to help me with what to say next. The conversation should have been an opportunity for Thomas to meaningfully evaluate his own learning.

Instead we sat awkwardly, waiting for me to say something.

The problem was that we had absolutely nothing to anchor our conversation. We had no clear vision about what his goals were as a learner, no clear understanding about the growth he was working toward. I had given my students the Common Core State Standards (CCSS) as a guide for their learning—about sixty-five standards in total. There were just too many to keep in the forefront of my instructional planning and their thinking about their work. Too many to guide the feedback I had shifted to in place of points. Too many to collect meaningful data that students could examine to determine what they had learned and where they had grown. We might as well have been operating without any learning goals at all.

The ironic thing is, I knew that my old points-based grading system would have saved me. I could have pulled up Thomas's records and pointed to all the places where the points he earned simply did not support an A grade. Even if the numbers didn't actually say much about what Thomas had learned and where he had grown, they would have proved to him that he had simply not collected enough points for the A.

But my students weren't collecting points to earn grades any more, and without a point system to define the rules of engagement, Thomas and I were drifting in the realm of our conflicting, fuzzy, unspoken assumptions about what an A or B looked like. When I stopped putting points and grades on my students' work, I removed the central focus of my classroom, but I did not carefully construct a new focus to replace it.

My experience that first semester taught me that it's not enough to just stop using points and grades. I needed a new foundation for my planning and to guide classroom feedback. I needed a focus for my data collection so my students could see clearly for themselves what they were learning. Sixty-five standards were just too many. I needed a set of clear and simple learning goals to keep us focused on what matters most.

In this chapter, I'll show you a process you can use to write your own learning goals for any course you teach. These goals will serve as the anchor you and your students will need to decide on final grades. This chapter will invite you to:

* Decide what you value most.

* Take a close look at what's required.

* Write a clear, simple list of learning goals for your classroom.

Decide What You Value Most

No matter how we approach grading, we can't cover everything that's required. Our lists of expected standards and curriculum objectives are too big, and students don't have time to read and write in depth if we're trying to cover everything. There simply isn't enough time, so we all make choices about what we will focus on and what we'll leave out.

The good news is, once we let go of feeling like we need to cover everything, we can shift our attention—and our students' attention—to the learning we value most. This learning becomes the foundation of our teaching, and it gives students a different and compelling purpose for their work once the need to collect points is gone.

I want my students to read books because it gives them practice in reading our complex world. There is no plot more complicated than life, no characters more confounding than actual human beings. Conflict, life's twists and turns, the complexity of human characters—we need practice in these things. Story gives us that practice. Reading books is an opportunity to try on the challenges of what it means to live a human life.

I want my students to practice writing so that they are able to write a future for themselves within all this human complexity. I want them to craft a voice, to contribute to the conversation, to pull together their stance and articulate it effectively no matter what the purpose or audience for their words. These values about why reading and writing matter for my students beyond the walls of my classroom are at the center of everything I do inside it.

The first step, then, in moving toward a different path to grades is to figure out where we want to go. We start by using the clearest, simplest language to articulate what it is we value *most* in our work with students. What is it that you want your students to learn and to be able to do with reading and writing in their lives beyond school? What is your richest vision for their success? In my own classroom, I can actually summarize this vision for my teaching in a single statement: Read the world to write your future.

Kelly Gallagher imagines a world where just four questions measure a teacher's effectiveness (2015, 188):

1. What percentage of your students can walk into a bookstore (or visit Goodreads.com) and know where to find books that interest them?

2. What percentage of your students write without being asked to do so by a teacher?

3. What percentage of your students can stand and speak effectively and confidently in front of a group of people?

4. What percentage of your students can actively listen to others—can carefully consider both what is said and what is not said?

Questions like these go straight to the heart of what we teach. No matter the grade or specific English language arts (ELA) curriculum, we're building readers, writers, and communicators. Distilling a vision for teaching into four essential questions or a single statement like "read the world to write your future" is important because it helps us find our teacher core. But we'll have to get much more specific as we move to craft goals that will guide our teaching. What values underlie students learning to read the world? What is worthy of students' attention if they are learning to write their future?

You know what matters to you about teaching reading and writing. It's the air you breathe. But just as fish don't really notice the water they swim in, your teaching values may be so implicit that they're actually difficult to put into words. However, you'll need words to help you design a classroom experience focused on student learning rather than points, so finding them is important.

Here are four questions that should help you articulate what you believe—regardless of curriculum requirements—is the most important learning students need to do as readers, writers, and thinkers. I invite you to write down your answers to these questions and maybe even talk about them with a colleague. Linger with them a while. After you've thought about the questions, use that thinking to help you generate a list of statements about what you value. Aim for concision. Look for overlap and where two statements might become one. The more focused your list, the better.

What brought you to teaching to begin with?

Think back to your shiny, new teacher idealism. What did that look like? What have you done to get closer and closer to realizing it in the time since those first days as a teacher?

We each have some specific motivation that brought us into the classroom. Maybe it was an awesome teacher you had who affected your life so significantly that you wanted to pay it forward. Or maybe you want to make sure your students don't experience what you went through as a student, and you hope to provide a richer, deeper, more personal experience. Or maybe it was some observation about the world that you thought teaching could help you address.

What have you picked up as you have observed your students from day to day?

Think about the individual moments from your classroom that have brought you more clarity. When have your students found the success that makes you feel that you chose the right career? When have things happened in your classroom that made you question your career decision? Where have your students struggled? Where have things turned out differently than you intended?

How have you come to a more simplified, focused understanding of what you're actually teaching?

Finding the essence of something—simplified—takes time and collaboration. I'm sure there have been individual classroom moments that have helped you think about what you really need to focus on in your classroom, but consider also how your thinking has been nudged by your colleagues—the teachers down the hall, and across the country, and in the books, blog posts, and journal articles you've read.

How do you want your classroom to help students to navigate the evolving literacy demands of our world?

The world we live in is constantly shifting and the changes have implications for our students' literacy. The skills we needed as high school graduates—even just a few years ago—are likely far less sophisticated than the skills our students need now. It's not enough to just be able to read and write. Students need to understand how to use different technologies effectively to communicate, how to make sense of multiple sources of information, and how to know when words are seeking to manipulate.

Take a Close Look at What's Required

As Jay McTighe (2012) reminds us, "Standards are not curriculum; they provide the framework upon which curricula are developed. Educators must translate Standards into a teachable curriculum." This translation process begins once you have a lean, clear list stating what you value. The next step is to see how your values line up with standards and requirements.

You'll need to gather your state standards, your course curriculum, your list of required texts, your writing scope and sequence—whatever documents there are that outline what you're supposed to teach. And don't forget the possibly unwritten expectations for the course as well. A specific vocabulary program? A list of literary terms? A particular pedagogy?

Now think carefully about what is actually required—not what's expected because it's always been done that way, but what is really, truly required. You know it's truly required if:

- ✴ Someone outside your classroom will evaluate your students on it. If you teach an Advanced Placement class, for instance, you must help students with the skills they'll need to be successful on the AP exam.

- ✴ Teachers within your building or across your district have agreed upon some common assessments for your course. You have to prepare your students for those assessments.

⁎ Your teacher evaluation assesses you based on a particular set of instructional strategies or mandates that you teach certain skills or content.

Anything else isn't actually required.

Making your way through that mass of documents may take a while, but once you've determined and listed what's actually required, compare it to your list of values as a teacher of reading and writing. Where are the lists the same? Where do they express the same general concept but with different words? Where are they different? As you study the two lists side by side, here are three things to keep in mind: language, scope, and conflict.

Navigating Obstacles 2.1

What if my school and/or district mandates common assessments or expects a group of teachers to be essentially on the same page?

It could be a powerful experience to go through the process in this chapter with a group of trusted colleagues. You could each work independently with the questions to discover your teaching values, and then talk about that process. You'll almost certainly discover commonalities, and you may be able to craft a shared vision to guide your decision-making about whatever it is that you're expected to do together. A strong, shared vision will also help you to push back at anything you decide collectively isn't good for your students as readers and writers.

Language

First, if there is a required standard or expectation that lines up with your values that you think might become one of your learning goals, consider whether you need to rewrite it. Most curriculum objectives weren't written with an audience of students in mind, so you may need to simplify the language. Find its essence. Make it a powerful statement that will speak to your students. For example, CCSS 9-10.2.D, "Use precise language and domain-specific vocabulary to manage the complexity of the topic and convey a style appropriate to the discipline and context as well as to the expertise of likely readers," could become, simply, "Whatever your topic, write like an insider" (National Governors Association Center for Best Practices and Council of Chief State School Officers 2010).

Scope

Often, it's easy to see how several requirements or standards might fit underneath a single broad value, sort of like an umbrella. For example, I want my students to make their own decisions about the form their writing needs to take depending on the needs of their intended audience and purpose. Though there is not an explicit standard about this in the CCSS, multiple writing standards actually relate to this value. I can think of my value as an umbrella goal that includes detail from several standards. I can access this detail whenever I need it for specific lesson planning, but the umbrella goal offers a much simpler, targeted focus.

Conflict

Finally, you'll need to figure out if there are any requirements that directly conflict with your values. If there are, I know it's tempting to leave them out, but you can't really just ignore what's required. Instead, consider how you might open a conversation that helps you either find some middle ground or resolve the conflict all together.

For years I was expected to teach specific, whole-class texts in most of my courses, but this conflicted directly with the choice I value so much as a reader and want for my students. Over time and in conversation with my colleagues, we worked to shift this requirement toward a balance of whole-class books (chosen by the teacher), small-group books, and independent choice books.

Resolution to conflicts may also come from adjusting something at the classroom level, like replacing a required weekly vocabulary quiz with a requirement that students include the words in the context of their writing. It may come from working with colleagues to study research-based best practice, or it may even require you to step beyond the walls of your school and sit on a committee to revise your district or state standards. Ultimately, the key to navigating any conflict between your values and what's required is having a strong, clear vision that guides your teaching because, as Katie Wood Ray (2001) explains, "I have to make my other curriculum responsibilities fit with [my vision], not the other way around" (189).

Write a Clear, Simple List of Learning Goals

After you've carefully studied the intersection between what you value and what's required, it's time to make decisions. For your classroom to orbit around learning instead of points, you'll need a short, simple list of clear goals that you and your students can focus on once the points and grades disappear. Assessment expert Rick Stiggins recommends no more than ten learning goals for any middle or high school class (2017, 52–53), and from my experience, I've found that to be pretty much the limit of what my students and I can hold in our heads consistently.

As you craft your list of learning goals, focus on describing what your students should do and become as a result of their experience in your class. I suggest you start with the stem, "The student" and then follow it with strong verbs and specific nouns that identify the work you want to see. You'll use the list to plan for instruction, to give you a focus for feedback, and to guide the data you collect in your grade book, but your students will use it too. As you'll see in Chapters 6 and 7, your students will use the list to craft learning goals for themselves, track their own progress and growth, and evaluate what they've learned at semester's end. Keep the language simple and direct and write with your students in mind.

To give you an example of what learning goals might look like for a single class, here are the ten goals that guide my senior ELA class (Figure 2.1). And to model the thinking outlined in this chapter, I've also included comments that will help you see how each goal came to be.

You may go through this process and end up with a list of learning goals that you could use for any ELA class that you teach. Or you may end up with a different list of goals for each course. It doesn't really matter. What's most important is that you explicate your values, discover what is actually required of your classroom, and then craft a short, simple list of learning goals to guide you and your students. In Online Resources 2.1 and 2.2, you'll find spreadsheets you can use as you move through this planning process.

Figure 2.1 An example of learning goals for one ELA class

Learning goal	Why this goal?	Nudges on my thinking	Connections to the CCSS
1. The student is a reader with a vibrant, self-directed reading practice that will continue beyond the classroom.	I've noticed too many of my students don't read books. But they need to.	• Penny Kittle's *Book Love* (2012) • Kelly Gallagher's *Readicide* (2009) • My own experiences as a reader in school	This is an umbrella learning goal for all the standards about reading. Unless students are actually reading, we can't focus on any of the skills outlined in the reading standards.
2. The student writes to think through life, to pull ideas together, to say something important to a targeted audience and for a specific purpose. The student is intentional about form and flexible to meet the changing needs of audience and purpose.	I've noticed my students sometimes ask for more specific prompts and example formats to structure their writing. But they need to struggle with critical decisions about form based on the needs of audience and purpose.	• Donald Graves • Penny Kittle's *Write Beside Them* (2008) • Kelly Gallagher's *Write Like This* (2011) • My own experiences as a writer in and out of school	This is an umbrella learning goal for several standards about writing: • Text Types and Purposes • Production of Writing • Range of Writing • Communication and Collaboration standards about audience and purpose • Presentation of Knowledge and Ideas standard about adapting when speaking to a variety of contexts and tasks • Standards about language and adapting language use to audience and purpose.

(continues)

Figure 2.1 An example of learning goals for one ELA class *(continued)*

Learning goal	Why this goal?	Nudges on my thinking	Connections to the CCSS
3. The student revises extensively to improve a piece of writing.	Students often think revising means only fixing mechanical errors. Or they write one draft and consider it done. I want to convince them that they will learn the most about writing during revision in response to feedback from readers.	• Ralph Fletcher's *What a Writer Needs* (1993) • Barry Lane's *After The End: Teaching and Learning Creative Revision* (1993) • Years of trying to get students to revise their work authentically	This goal rewrites and simplifies one standard below "Production of Writing" that includes revision.
4. The student asks complex questions and persists to research answers to them.	I worry about what the internet is doing to our brains. I need to help students wade through all of the information at their fingertips and persist through complexity to figure things out.	• *The Shallows* by Nicolas Carr (2011) • Observing my own struggles with navigating the presence of the internet in my life • *Deep Work: Rules for Focused Success in a Distracted World* by Cal Newport (2016)	This is an umbrella learning goal that covers standards below "Research to Build Present Knowledge" and standards about reading.
5. The student seeks out mentor texts—for writing, for text form, for thinking, for reading—and uses those mentor texts to grow.	My students become more independent as writers, readers, and thinkers when they can seek out and study their own mentor texts.	• Allison Marchetti and Rebekah O'Dell's *Writing with Mentors* (2015) • My own work with mentor texts as I write • My work with the Colorado Writing Project	This is an umbrella learning goal that covers standards about close reading of a variety of texts as well as the writing standards under "Production and Distribution of Writing."

Learning goal	Why this goal?	Nudges on my thinking	Connections to the CCSS
6. The student maintains a writer's notebook as an important thinking and reflecting space.	Humans need to sit with their thoughts, push on them, explore them. We need to keep track of what we think about what we read, what we might want to write about, what we're learning.	• Penny Kittle's *Write Beside Them* (2008) • Linda Rief's *Read, Write, Teach* (2014) • My own work with a writer's notebook • Stevi Quate's work with teachers on writer's notebooks that she has curated on her "Writing Workshop Basics" website	This is an umbrella learning goal for the standards below "Range of Writing."
7. The student takes risks to learn.	Life has taught me that we learn more when we take risks. I want to work explicitly with my students on this and take risks myself alongside them to show them what it looks like.	• Alfie Kohn's "The Case Against Grades" (2011) • Liz Prather's *Project-Based Writing* (2017) • My own risk-taking as a student and a teacher	This goal goes beyond the CCSS.

(continues)

Figure 2.1 An example of learning goals for one ELA class *(continued)*

Learning goal	Why this goal?	Nudges on my thinking	Connections to the CCSS
8. The student is a positive community member: provides high-quality feedback to peers on their writing, participates earnestly in small-group and whole-group conversations, moves through our classroom spaces (physical and digital) with kindness.	Learning is about relationship. People will take risks to learn when surrounded by people who make them feel safe. And as a community, we need to share the task of providing feedback.	• My own realization that I can't provide all the feedback my students need on their writing • Years of working to build community to support my students as readers and writers • Umpteen conference presentations attended over the years about building community in the classroom • Liz Prather's *Project-Based Writing* (2017)	This is an umbrella learning goal for the "Speaking and Listening" standards.
9. The student demonstrates successful student habits: meeting deadlines, reading and following instructions, asking questions, seeking help and support, and managing digital tools and digital spaces effectively to keep track of work.	Do they read instructions? Do they pay attention to details? Do they respect deadlines? Why do they sometimes struggle and not ask for help?	• *Creating Self-Regulated Learners* by Linda Nilson (2013) • Observations of my students' inability to demonstrate successful student habits	This goal goes beyond the CCSS.

Learning goal	Why this goal?	Nudges on my thinking	Connections to the CCSS
10. The student practices effective self-reflection, self-evaluation, and meta-cognition. Students know what they already know, what they want and need to know, what they've learned, and how well they've learned it.	Students should be their own judges about what they've learned or haven't learned and where they have grown rather than waiting for points in a grade book to tell them.	• *Creating Self-Regulated Learners* by Linda Nilson (2013) • Alfie Kohn's "The Case Against Grades" (2011) • My district's Educator Effectiveness Standards that call on us to create classrooms where students use feedback to improve and monitor learning and assume ownership for evaluating and monitoring their progress • John Hattie's (2008) list of factors related to student achievement with "student self-reported grades" as the second most influential factor	This goal goes beyond the CCSS.

From experience I can also tell you that your list of learning goals will evolve and become more precise as you continue to work with the goals and teach from them. Even as I've been writing this chapter, I've made some tweaks to my goals, getting me closer to the clear vision that I want to sit at the center of my classroom. But it's a work in progress, and my aim is for it to be compelling enough and focused enough that both my students and I can keep it at the forefront of our work together.

With a list of learning goals in hand, the next step is to make sure that what you ask your students to do in your class aligns with those goals. What will they need to practice? What specific tasks will you ask of them? What will a daily and weekly routine look like? The next chapter walks you through a process to move from your goals to designing the work of the classroom.

Interlude

Semester Grade Letter by Ella, Grade 6, English Language Arts

Dear Mrs. Breed,

Ella feels like she has changed course over the school year. She was driving on the highway, not caring for the many exits. Now, she feels she is better at paying attention to not just the road, but the small differences in each route. Now, she pays more attention to the journey, instead of only thinking about the destination. Life is too short to be thinking about the future.

Ella chooses to write the story of her learning in the third person, something I also invite my students to do if they wish.

In the beginning of the road trip, Ella could read. Just that, she could read. She would scan the page, imagine the characters, but never ask questions. "It's a waste of time!" she would say to herself, "why ask questions if they will be answered further on in the book?" Now, Ella understands the importance of asking questions, and not just any questions, the right questions. She can now infer, and have a better chance of being correct. Ella has improved very much this year within the subject of reading, and is looking forward to reading all summer.

Ella has chosen a metaphor to anchor her story: her learning journey as a road trip.

Ella never had too much trouble with writing, except for one big problem. She couldn't make a story last. No matter how much she added to the plot, her "chapter books" only took about ten minutes to read. In the first and second semester, Ella learned more about "show, don't tell" this is an example of Ella's writing in the beginning of the year, ". . . She was sad. She hadn't expected her time in Desolation to go by this fast. . . ." This is an example of what Ella changed it to, later in the year, " . . . Her eyes held mine, the sadness of the scenario seeping through our pupils, as tears escaped their prison, 'I didn't expect this to all be over, our time on Desolation wasn't nearly enough . . .' she sobbed." As you see, Ella improved in lengthening the story, and in showing what the character was feeling, instead of telling about it.

You'll notice in Monica's instructions that she reminds her students of the target skills they worked on during the year. "Inferring strategy" is on the list.

This is not one of the particular writing skills listed in Monica's instructions. Ella has created her own target for growth in her writing, which shows the agency she has over her own work. Nested within Ella's goal is one that Monica listed, "using 'show don't tell.'" But Ella has framed that skill within a larger goal she has for herself as a writer.

Ella never had trouble with speaking aloud, she never got too nervous about it. She never understood stage fright. The worst thing that could really happen, she would say to herself, is getting too nervous, and ruining the whole role she was playing. The road was seemingly endless, for the learning went on forever. But, even when Ella thought she knew everything there is to know about speaking, she learned more. She learned how, if you just start talking, no one is really going to listen. You have to reel the audience in. You must project your voice, in order to ensure you are heard. You must share your creations, no matter how "embarrassing" it may seem, before someone else does. If you want to be known, first, you must know yourself, and how to have a good stage presence.

Over the course of the school year, Ella took way more U-turns, to really understand the road. This is something she never would have done in the beginning of this road trip, and Ella believes that you, Mrs. Breed were auto piloting throughout the whole ride. Ella thinks she has earned an A– this semester, for she has demonstrated her growth, and her new attention to the road.

—Ella

Monica Breed teaches sixth grade in a middle school in my district. Take a look at her instructions in Online Resource 7.2 to see her smart scaffolding of this task for her students. She provides clear and concise instructions, a reminder to students to focus on the "growth moves" they discussed during the semester, and a table that pulls together the skills the class targeted to help students with ideas for what to write about.

Chapter Three

Plan the Work Students Will Do

EARLY IN MY TEACHING CAREER, MY STUDENTS PRODUCED A LOT OF writing that I never asked them to revisit for any meaningful purpose. They would write. I would grade. We would move on. I hadn't yet figured out how to make space in my classroom for revision.

But I knew that revision was important, so I began a quest to get my students to revise their writing.

I thought if I asked to see rough *and* final drafts they would revise.

They turned in two identical drafts stapled together.

To emphasize that a rough draft should be different from a final draft, I asked them to use a highlighter to point out what was different between the two drafts.

They made pretend rough drafts. They cut out a paragraph or two from the paper, created a few errors, highlighted those differences, printed the fake "rough draft" and stapled it to the paper to comply with my request.

Then I thought that maybe I could trick students into doing actual rough and final drafts. So, I called their papers "final drafts" but gave feedback along with the grade and invited them to revise. I thought I was so clever when I announced as I handed back their papers, "This grade is *not* final. If you're not happy with it, I invite you to revise to bring up your grade!"

They looked over the rubric and determined the shortest, easiest path to collecting the points needed to get the grade they wanted. Usually the easiest path was to fix the errors I had highlighted.

This of course is copyediting, not revision. And only a handful of them even chose to do this minimal work.

To be truthful, I understood my students because I used to do the same thing in college. I believed I did my best work under the last-minute pressure of a deadline—until I once wrote a paper two weeks before it was due. I'm not sure why I did, but working on the paper shattered my notion that I did my best work at the last minute. The paper I ended up with was a thing of beauty. It glowed and sparkled as it sat there on my desk, neatly stapled to a fresh title page. I knew it shined because of how many times I had looked over it, how many things I had added or cut or reworked or moved around. I was so proud of that paper. I learned that I did my best work when I revised.

I wanted my students to learn what I had learned about revision, but the work I was asking them to do just wasn't leading them there. My students were only copyediting, and most of them weren't even doing that. The problem was, I was emphasizing typical classroom products: rough and final drafts, scored for a grade on a rubric. The focus I created wasn't on the process, the work, the writing. It was about producing pieces of paper that appeared to have met the specifications on the rubric to determine how many points to put in the grade book. My students took the easiest possible path to completing the task, and they weren't really learning anything about revision.

In the years since I moved away from points-based grading, I've challenged myself to make the process of revision itself the focus, rather than emphasizing the products of writing. I crafted a clear and simple goal to capture this shift—"The student revises extensively to improve a piece of writing"—and I knew it was paying off when a student tried to bribe me with something from Starbucks if I agreed that her revision was complete. She and I had gone back and forth on a piece of writing several times. Each time I asked her to revisit the way she was connecting her examples to her claims, and each time she did something minimal. She never really dug in to figure out what my feedback was asking her to think about.

Rather than accepting the bribe, I sat with her in the computer lab with her draft up on the screen and talked through my feedback, her intentions, and her path forward with revision. Finally, she did some authentic revision work. The bribe attempt suggested to me that the task was challenging her to do the actual work of revision, which is hard and messy, but it's the struggle that writers must engage. Having a clear learning goal about revision changed how I invited students to revise and created space for them to do authentic revision work.

The shift from a focus on products to a focus on process changes everything. Because the grading system expects us to hold students accountable for doing the work of the curriculum, we organize courses around the products that work well as traditional accountability measures—exams, papers, presentations—that we can assess with points and rubrics. This places an emphasis on product over process, often obscuring our students' understanding of authentic reading and writing. They focus on earning maximum rubric points rather than on the messy, frustrating process that humans confront in writing. They read books to earn points on reading quizzes, or to do well on big exams, or to have enough to say to write adequate essays in response to prompts we design for them.

But learning *lives* in the process, in the work that writers and readers do along the way. Once we let go of points and rubrics, we can design a completely different classroom experience by remembering that our students—and their individual journeys to become readers and writers—are the ultimate product. The process of their learning becomes the focus, and the work we ask them to do aligns seamlessly with our learning goals. That's what this chapter will lead you to do:

- ✱ Consider the mismatch between tasks focused on products and learning goals.

- ✱ Determine what students need to practice to meet learning goals.

- ✱ Repurpose traditional accountability measures to better support readers and writers.

- ✱ Imagine new possibilities that hold students accountable for learning.

- ✱ Set up routines that protect the work students need to do.

Consider the Mismatch Between Tasks Focused on Products and Learning Goals

As teachers, we always have the best intentions when we design tasks for students, but a closer look shows how some fairly common classroom tasks don't invite the kind of focused work our learning goals suggest. As an example, take a look at the rubric and revision task for a paper on Jon Krakauer's *Into the Wild* that I used in my classroom several years ago (Figure 3.1). I've annotated it to point out the mismatch between the task and several of my learning goals (detailed in the last chapter), including the one about revision, which it was meant to target.

My intentions for the *Into the Wild* task were honorable. I crafted some specific statements to define the task that would give students something to focus on as they worked. I made a clear key to show what the numbers meant and how I would use them to calculate the grade. I gave students some power to increase the grade by rewriting if they chose to. But in addition to the mismatch with the learning goals I

Figure 3.1 Rubric for the compare-and-contrast essay on *Into the Wild* (80 points)

Category	Expectations	Teacher Evaluation
Ideas and Content	• The essay focuses on a significant aspect of Krakauer's *Into the Wild* and compares and contrasts it to some other significant idea/topic within or beyond the text. • A clear thesis is present. • The essay is focused; it does not try to accomplish too much. • The essay presents strong, compelling evidence to support its claims.	
Organization	• The introduction is inviting and original, and it captures the attention of the reader. In other words, you draw the reader into your writing. • Overall organization is clear/straightforward, following either the subject-by-subject compare-and-contrast organization or the point-by-point compare-and-contrast organization. • The conclusion is meaningful and brings the paper to a satisfying end.	
Voice	• The writer demonstrates a clear knowledge of purpose, audience, and form for this assignment (i.e., the voice is appropriate for the task). • The voice is genuine and authentic. It's *you*.	
Conventions	• Obvious errors should not be distracting. • Polished draft follows MLA format for heading, line spacing, and page numbers. • Includes a correctly formatted works cited page referencing the primary source (*Into the Wild*) and any other sources you may have used in the paper.	
	Average Score	

Both here and in the key and grade scale below the rubric, I spell out clearly how the score will impact a student's grade. This makes it difficult for students to take risks to learn (Goal 7). Because the rubric category scores will average into a grade that will then go in as up to 80 points in the grade book, the results of this writing task are high stakes. Students will play it safe. Risks aren't worth it if there are real consequences to the constantly being calculated grade.

The rubric directs the writing task narrowly. Though there is some room for choice here, the compare-and-contrast entry point might not be the best invitation for all students. This impedes their opportunity to use the shared text as an invitation to ask complex questions that matter and persist to research answers to them (Goal 4).

The rubric indicates only two possible organizational structures. This removes the need for students to make some important writerly decisions and to be intentional about form and flexible to meet the changing needs of the audience and purpose (Goal 2).

Figure 3.1 *Continued*

Key:	Scale:
4 = awesome!	3.5–4 = A
3 = good; room for growth	2.5–3.4 = B
2 = missing something	1.5–2.4 = C
1 = made an attempt	0.5–1.4 = D

Want to rewrite? Go for it!!!!

1. Make your changes on this document.

2. Leave my comments there so I can see what I thought before your revisions.

3. Highlight your changes so that I don't miss a single thing that you made different in your revision.

   ✶ If you cut something out, insert a comment to tell me what you cut out.

4. Resubmit by the rewrite due date.

   ✶ The new grade will go into the grade book (unless it's lower than the original score).

> *My invitation to rewrite is only optional. If I'm serious about all students revising extensively, this won't get me there (Goal 3). Also, the narrowly defined task and the offer of only two possible organizational structures really constrict what is possible for students in revision. There's not much room for them to grow.*

noted in the task description, the assignment didn't require students to work toward other important goals, for example, using mentor texts to grow as writers (Goal 5) or giving feedback to each other on their writing (Goal 8). This task added up to a lot of missed opportunities for my students to do the writing and revision work outlined by my learning goals.

Determine What Students Need to Practice to Meet Learning Goals

I've learned that to design tasks for a class, I have to think first about exactly what students need to practice to move toward the learning goals I have for the course, and then from there, I identify what I will ask students to do to engage in that practice. The goal, of course, is to find tasks rich enough to encompass multiple learning goals, but it helps to start the process with a single goal clearly in mind. Let's consider both those steps now, and as an example, I'll stay focused on my learning goal about revision, "The student revises extensively to improve a piece of writing."

In the *Into the Wild* task, my optional invitation for students to revise to bring up their grade didn't lead them to revise extensively to improve their writing. Practice in revision requires so much more than fixing errors or producing fake rough drafts. I want students reconsidering how they've put the whole piece of writing together. I want them reworking sentences, moving ideas around, striking out entire paragraphs. I want my students to choose the best way to craft their words to say exactly what they want them to say for a particular audience and a particular reason to write. This kind of revision is what writers beyond school actually do, and it's the kind of revision I want my students to practice.

If my goal is "extensive" revision, students will need help staying engaged, and working on revising the writing that matters most to them will help with engagement. But students will need guidance as they practice choosing which pieces of writing to revise. What should they consider? How do they know which piece has the potential to help them most as writers?

Students will also need to practice the tools and strategies of revision, beginning with rereading and reconsidering. They'll need practice putting their writing in the hands of readers, giving the feedback most needed, and determining which feedback to use as they revise. They'll also need to practice finding appropriate mentor texts and using them to inspire revision.

Navigating Obstacles 3.1

I'm worried that I don't have time to reinvent all my assignments.

Good news! You don't have to. With a little thoughtful repurposing, many of the assessment tools you currently use will serve your learning goals just as well.

I have to plan intentionally for all of this practice to happen and create tasks that ensure it happens. To this end, I now ask my students to extensively revise one or two pieces of writing per semester. Students use feedback from me and their peers in the revision process, and they seek guidance from mentor texts as well. Each time they turn the writing back in to me for additional feedback, they explain their revision decisions in a memo. I try to talk about this assignment in a way that emphasizes the process instead of the final product. The point of the task is the work itself—to get students fully involved in authentic revision to reach the end goal of growing writers who revise. (See Figure 3.2.)

The thorough revision assignment continues to evolve as I learn from my students' experiences with it, and every tweak either aligns the assignment more closely with the goal or encompasses more goals in the process. In addition to extensive revision, for example, this assignment also enables my students to work toward nearly all of the course's other learning goals, making it a good candidate for some of the major work my students must complete to get credit for the class. Not every bit of work we ask of students needs to address every learning goal, but students do need opportunities to work toward every learning goal.

Figure 3.2 Guidelines for thorough revision

To get a thorough revision marked as *complete* in the grade book, you'll need to do the following:

> *The thorough revision assignment is required of all students, so they can't opt out of revising (Goal 3).*

1. Choose one of the drafts you've completed—the one you think has the most potential, the one you really want to honor with some revision work.

2. Get some inspiration for revision:
   * reader feedback
   * mentor text
   * or both.

> *The emphasis on numbers, scores, and grades is gone. Students keep working until they learn what they can from the piece of writing. The eventual "complete" (after possibly several rounds of revision) is not a grade—just an indicator that the work on this task is complete. It is safe for students to take risks; there is no grade penalty if they try something that doesn't work out (Goal 7).*

3. Start revising. Do *all* revisions in suggesting mode on the original Google Doc.

4. Capture your thinking about your revision work with a revision memo written at the end:
   * What did you do in revision? What did you focus on; what were the most significant changes you made? Why did you make them?
   * How did your revision inspiration help you revise?
     * What did your readers say and how did you use that feedback?

   and/or

     * How did the mentor text help you with revision?
   * Which of your individual learning goals did your revision work help you with?
   * What work remains on this piece?

> *The writing is not narrowly defined. After completing a few different drafts, students choose the one they want to revise. This enables them to say something important to a targeted audience for a specific purpose (Goal 2).*

> *Students are asked to seek inspiration for revision via feedback from readers (Goal 8), by studying a mentor text (Goal 5), or by doing both.*

5. Turn in (by the deadline!).

6. Wait for your teacher to return it to you with more possible revision work.
   * If it's marked *partial*, *keep at it*, or *almost*, go back to step 1 and repeat the whole process.
   * If it's marked *complete*, you're done!

> *Chapter 5 will discuss how I use these terms in my grade book.*

> *Students complete a memo at the end explaining their revision work where they connect the work to their individual learning goals, enabling the student to practice effective self-reflection, self-evaluation, and metacognition (Goal 10).*

To design the work of a course so it helps students meet the learning goals you've established, start by asking yourself, "What—exactly—does it look like if a student is doing what this goal suggests?" Then, make bulleted lists of the specific behaviors students need to practice in service of each goal. You'll use these lists to imagine the assignments that will get your students engaged in the work that really matters.

Repurpose Traditional Accountability Measures to Better Support Readers and Writers

As you begin to imagine the work students need to do toward your learning goals, you don't need to start totally from scratch and create completely new tasks. Start by examining what you already have in place to see how well it lines up with your learning goals. In some cases, you can keep right on asking students to do those tasks. In other cases, you might need to repurpose them.

For example, take one of the most common traditional accountability measures found in an English language arts classroom—the reading quiz. Teachers use quizzes to make sure students are reading and to check how well they are understanding what they read. Because quizzes are frequent, they need to be short and easy to grade, so the format is typically multiple choice, short answer, or true or false. But when students' scores on a reading quiz calculate into the ever-present grade that the grade book spits out, that quiz can feel like it's high stakes. Students may take shortcuts to ensure they can answer the questions without putting in the hard work of reading and understanding the texts we put in front of them. And of course, sometimes students do fine on graded reading quizzes without actually reading the text itself, so the resulting data distort what they reflect.

Once I moved away from points-based grading, rather than give up problematic reading quizzes, I decided to repurpose them so the score isn't high stakes and the focus shifts to learning. I retitled them "reading comprehension checks," and students still get scores, but the score doesn't calculate into the overall grade the grade book constantly generates (Chapter 5 will suggest some ways to do this). Instead, the score becomes part of the data record in the grade book and students can see it when they self-evaluate their learning at different points in the semester (much more on this in Chapter 6). But it's only a data point, not a high-stakes measure.

Why does this matter? Well, there's no reason for students to take shortcuts to get the grade if the score *isn't* a grade. Cheating no longer gets students anywhere useful. There's no more quibbling over points lost for the overspecific questions I end up writing even when I'm trying not to. Most importantly, the reading comprehension check can become a learning tool for students.

With a reading comprehension check instead of a reading quiz, students can evaluate their own comprehension. They can discuss the answers with their peers since the score isn't a high-stakes grade. And depending on how you set up the task (I'm a fan of Google Form quizzes that score themselves and give students immediate feedback on which questions they got right and wrong), students can do the reading comprehension check as many times as they want until they get the right answers.

Navigating Obstacles 3.2

What if you're required to use particular exams or quizzes?

Use them, but list the score in the grade book so it's data you and your students can see, but it doesn't calculate into the overall grade.

I teach on a team of Advanced Placement (AP) Lit teachers, and not everyone is approaching grades the same way. We did, however, all agree to use the same literary terms exam for the first semester final. My students took it just like all the other AP Lit students did, and they prepared for it just as much and as well, but in the end, the score was a data point instead of a grade. Both my students and I used the data point to make decisions about next steps in the course. The whole process of preparing for, taking, and reviewing how they did on the exam became an important part of their journeys to grow as readers.

Every bit of conversation students are having with each other about what happened in a text, every bit of reviewing students are doing about the critical moments in a text—these things are a win. Students are getting to know the text better. The reading quiz morphs from a product—an end in itself—to a tool that helps students in their process to grow as readers.

My reading comprehension checks have evolved over time, too, and I've found that if I add on a few reading process questions (How much time did you spend reading this text? How carefully did you read? Where did you struggle?), then the check serves two additional important purposes: self-reflection for students and data I can use to plan my next steps of instruction. When students know there are no high stakes attached to their answers, they are more likely to be honest, providing the data that will be most helpful. I need to know if students didn't read and why they didn't read. I need to know where they struggled. I need to know what is really going on with readers to best support their growth. High-stakes accountability measures don't give me this kind of information.

Another bonus to repurposing reading quizzes is that you can design what will best serve your students' learning without worrying about generating the kind of data that you can turn into a grade. For example, my AP Lit students finish out the year with Toni Morrison's *Beloved*, a very challenging text to understand due to the constant invasion of the past on the present storyline in the text. Hence, the reading comprehension check I designed for them presented a list of plot events as they appear in each chapter and asked students to simply check off which plot events happen in the present timeline of the book.

My students audibly groaned when I explained how I had structured the comprehension check, suggesting I had hit what they were struggling with most as they read. They used the reading comprehension check to assist with their understanding as they read the book. They could go to it after reading a chapter, review the plot details, and see if they had kept the past and present events straight. As they did this, I had a constant stream of useful data coming at me that showed how the reading was going for them and identified students who were struggling and needed more support.

With your learning goals in front of you, take some time to consider how the accountability tasks and measures you are already using do and do not help move students toward those goals. Knowing that not everything needs to end with points and grades, are there ways you might repurpose some of them to shift the emphasis and better support your students as learners?

Imagine New Possibilities That Hold Students Accountable for Learning

Readers and writers need authentic reasons to work, and when you're not focused so much on the kinds of products that are easy to score with points, there's an entire world of new possibilities out there. It's wonderfully liberating to think about: Free of the constraints of grading, what authentic assignments and assessments might be possible? What is your richest vision for the work students might do in your classroom?

Let's start with reading. What if you asked students to read a book so they could have a conversation with you about it? Not for an exam or to write a paper, but to sit in a small group of classmates who had also read the book and just *talk* about it.

What if you gave students the questions ahead of time so they could reflect: What do you think the text argues about the human experience? How does it make that argument? Is it a true statement about life? If so, how does it change you as a human being? (Edmundson 2002). What if you used conferences and informal writing along the way to help students focus their thinking on the questions and get ready for the conversation?

Can you imagine a conversation that feels like you're sitting around the dinner table talking about life, inspired by a book assigned in school, and just because you said you would be having the conversation? You could participate in the conversation as a fellow reader since you wouldn't have to worry about doling out points and evaluating what students say. You could listen to see what you might learn about your students' growth as readers. And the conversation models the kinds of conversations students could have with people about books for the rest of their lives.

This is the kind of classroom activity that builds readers, but the moment you start awarding points for something like this, it loses its power. In this case, it would no longer be a group of readers having a meaningful conversation about a shared text. It would be a group of students competing with one another for points, saying the things they think the teacher wants to hear. When you approach grades differently, however, a structure like this becomes possible.

Now let's think about writing. For years I struggled through stacks of papers, especially the big, culminating, end-of-semester ones, alone. I had to determine a grade on each paper to figure into students' final grades. I spent a lot of my grading energy justifying the points I took off based on a rubric. It was exhausting, and I always worried that it sent the wrong message to students for me to be the only audience for a piece of writing that supposedly reflected the culmination of their work for an entire semester.

Now that I don't put points and grades on individual pieces of writing, I've been able to invite students to do much more authentic activities with their writing. For example, last year my students wrote magazine-style feature pieces about topics they chose. We spent an entire semester on the feature genre—unpacking how it weaves together both narrative and informational writing into one complex, engaging text. We read and studied mentor texts. We discovered ideas. My students wrote and revised and wrote and revised some more as I worked alongside them, offering feedback and conversation to help them craft a piece that met their goals.

Only a few years ago, the end game with these feature pieces would have been a final draft that I scored with a rubric, but letting all that go helped me imagine totally new possibilities. I challenged my students to become the staff of a magazine, organized into sections, with a pair of co–editors in chief who figured out what the overall focus of their magazine would be. The students in each section had to read each other's features to figure out why they had been grouped together (providing feedback for yet more revision in the process) so they could design a cover page for their section. They worked together to lay out their sections using free, online design software. I pulled their sections into one PDF with the cover page that the co–editors in chief designed.

And even the final version of the magazine wasn't our end point. For the final exam, each student was assigned to read one other student's feature, write a letter in response, and then use that letter as an entrance ticket into a Socratic Seminar using their class magazine as the text up for discussion. Each student got an extensive, personalized response—from a peer, which is often more valuable to them than from their teacher. The class worked together to create something they were proud of having made, and the final exam conversation became a real celebration of their work.

My hope is that this chapter has helped you to think about this important question: If you didn't have to evaluate everything your students did for the purpose of putting points in the grade book, what kinds of authentic assignments and assessments might be possible? For each of your learning goals, consider the following questions:

- ✶ What practice will students need to accomplish the learning goal?
- ✶ What work will you ask students to do?
- ✶ Which of your traditional accountability measures could you repurpose to serve your learning goals?
- ✶ What new, more authentic tasks can you imagine asking your students to do?

Figure 3.3 shows how I've answered these questions based on the learning goals you've seen in this chapter and in Chapter 2. My hope is that sharing my answers in this much detail will help you imagine the progression from goals to practice to tasks in your own course.

Figure 3.3 How I plan the work my students will do

Learning Goal	Students will have to practice	So I will ask this work of them
1. The student is a reader with a vibrant, self-directed reading practice that will continue beyond my classroom.	• Reading. Actually reading. Not fake reading. Regularly—every day even • Forming positive associations with reading • Choosing texts on their own • Abandoning texts when necessary • Making plans for themselves as readers	• Read one or two books together as a class (high-interest titles only). • Read several books independently that they choose on their own. • Let me know each week how the reading is going (weekly reading check-in Google Form). • Talk to me about their reading in individual and group conferences. • Read silently in class for at least 10 minutes every day.
2. The student writes to think through life, to pull ideas together, to say something important to a targeted audience and for a specific purpose. The student is intentional about form and flexible to meet the changing needs of audience and purpose.	• Making decisions about writing—what they want to say, to whom they want to say it, why they want to say it, what form the writing should take to meet those intentions • Choosing topics that are relevant and important to them so they will stick with the writing	• Write something of their own design (guided by curriculum expectations) every week. • Talk with me about their writing in conferences. • Talk with their peers about their writing. • Work on a major semester piece of writing that they choose the topic for and determine the form based on their intentions for the piece. • Articulate their purposes and process on every piece of writing with a writer's memo.

Learning Goal	Students will have to practice	So I will ask this work of them
3. The student revises extensively to improve a piece of writing.	• Reworking pieces of writing several times • Choosing which pieces to work on so they can direct their efforts toward work that most engages them • Seeking reader feedback and/or mentor texts to get ideas for revision	• Thoroughly revise one to two pieces of writing per semester, going back and forth with me (feedback/revision/repeat) several times. • Work with peers to gain strategies for revision. • Study mentor texts to gain strategies for revision. • Articulate in writer's memos the decisions made in revision.
4. The student asks complex questions and persists to research answers to them.	• Discovering what they are interested in exploring • Writing questions that are worth researching • Finding credible sources • Understanding source bias • Collecting and keeping track of research sources and documenting them in writing • Writing reflectively to make sense of what they are discovering • Research strategies: interviewing, database searching, observations, etc.	• Determine a topic for the major semester piece of writing early in the semester so they can make as many reading and writing decisions as possible toward continued work on that topic. • Write a major semester piece of writing that is research-based. • Correctly cite research sources.
5. The student seeks out mentor texts—for writing, for text form, for thinking, for reading—and uses those mentor texts to grow.	• Using a mentor text to develop and revise a piece of writing • Finding mentor texts that will help a reader/writer grow	• Seek out mentor texts as inspiration for writing and/or revision and write about how they used them in writer's memos. • Collect mentor texts that are most meaningful to them.

(continues)

Figure 3.3 How I plan the work my students will do *(continued)*

Learning Goal	Students will have to practice	So I will ask this work of them
6. The student maintains a writer's notebook as an important thinking and reflecting space.	• Setting up, using, and maintaining a writer's notebook • Different strategies for writer's notebook work: collecting, thinking, discovering topics for writing, lists (of books to read, big ideas, moments of failure, etc.), reflection, tracking learning, setting goals, etc.	• Acquire a writer's notebook at the start of the semester and use it in class every day. • Share with peers their favorite writer's notebook pages so they can get ideas for writer's notebook strategies from each other. • Show me work in their writer's notebooks periodically.
7. The student takes risks to learn.	• Contributing ideas in class discussion • Going beyond any formulas they've been taught for writing • Finding texts to read that will stretch and challenge them	• Participate in Socratic Seminars and discuss in small groups and with the whole class. • Choose topics to write about and texts to read that will challenge them. • Study mentor texts to discover new possibilities for their writing.
8. The student is a positive community member: provides high-quality feedback to peers on their writing, participates earnestly in small-group and whole-group conversations, moves through our classroom spaces (physical and digital) with kindness.	• Giving helpful feedback to peers on their writing • Keeping small-group conversation on focus • Contributing thoughtfully to whole-class conversations • Listening carefully • Getting to know classmates • Kindness	• Discuss what makes for helpful feedback to writers. • Leave marginal notes on peers' writing so I can see how they're doing giving feedback. • Talk frequently in small groups and reflect on how well they maintained focus in those groups. • Choose to listen or participate in Socratic Seminars. • Participate in some icebreaker/community building activities. • Be kind. Always.

Learning Goal	Students will have to practice	So I will ask this work of them
9. The student demonstrates successful student habits: meeting deadlines, reading and following instructions, asking questions, seeking help and support, and managing digital tools and digital spaces effectively to keep track of work.	• Using Google Classroom, Gmail, and the electronic grade book to monitor their work for class • Reading instructions for assignments and paying close attention to details	• Turn in all work via Google Classroom. • Monitor Gmail for class-related things. • Resubmit assignments that show they did not carefully follow instructions. • Read my instructions carefully and explain why they are important and how they help me to manage the work of all of my 155 students.
10. The student practices effective self-reflection, self-evaluation, and metacognition. Students know what they already know, what they want and need to know, what they've learned, and how well they've learned it.	• Choosing target learning goals, determining their baseline for each goal, monitoring progress, and reflecting on what they've learned • Figuring out how they'll pursue their learning goals and track their own progress and growth.	• Choose individual learning goals from the list of learning goals for the course and reflect to monitor their progress. • Map out a plan to follow for their learning goals. • Complete self-evaluations of growth for each six-week grading period. • Write at the end of the semester to describe and document the growth achieved and determine a semester grade that best captures that growth.

Set Up Routines That Protect the Work Students Need to Do

Once you have a clear idea about what you're teaching (defined by a list of learning goals), and you've figured out what work you'll ask your students to do, the next step is to structure a routine to protect the time and space your students will need to do that work.

We only have so much time with our students each week, and as the planners of the time, we control how our students will spend it, so we have to be very intentional. In *180 Days* (2018), Kelly Gallagher and Penny Kittle sketch out their similar daily routines that protect time for reading, writer's notebook writing, minilessons, and work on evolving drafts of writing (26–27). They start the book outlining the beliefs that underpin their teaching, and those beliefs drive the daily routine. They say that no matter the grade level of students they work with, the routine would be the same, "sound instructional practice for readers and writers of all ages" (27).

As I plan for instruction in my classroom each week, I think about this idea that my beliefs shape routines. I've devised a weekly, rather than daily, routine that protects time and space for the work outlined in my learning goals. (See Figure 3.4.)

Figure 3.4 How my weekly routine supports students in the practice that serves my learning goals.

Monday (50 min)	1. Time to read (10 min) 2. Grade book check-in and learning goal progress update (5 min) 3. Mentor text study and practice in writer's notebooks (40 min)
Tuesday (50 min)	1. Time to read (includes weekly reading check-in) (10 min) 2. Time to write (includes meeting with peer response groups and teacher conferences as needed and debriefing the writing time at the end of class) (40 min)
Wednesday/ Thursday (90 min) (half of classes each day)	1. Time to read (10 min) 2. Reading response group conversation (10 min) 3. Writing minilesson (10–20 min) 4. Time to write (includes meeting with peer response groups and teacher conferences as needed and debriefing the writing time at the end of class) (50–60 min) • Weekly draft due by end of class
Friday (50 min)	1. Time to read (10 min) 2. Whole-class discussion on texts we're reading or looking at texts we're writing (40 min)

Daily time to read helps students establish regular reading practices (Goal 1).

Every week I ask students to look over the grade book data I've collected and then reflect on their learning goal progress (more on this in Chapter 6). Doing this on a Monday helps students set goals for the week (Goal 10).

Weekly mentor text study together as a class shows students how to use mentor texts and helps them build their own reserves of mentor texts to consult (Goal 5).

In weekly directed writer's notebook work, students learn strategies for thinking and reflecting and establish practices they can engage in on their own (Goal 6).

Large chunks of time to write enable students to sink into their writing and thinking as well as provide time for peer response, teacher conferences, individual mentor text study, individual writer's notebook work, and revision work (Goals 2, 3, 4, 5, 6, 8).

Response groups make risk-taking safe (Goal 7) as students try out ideas in small groups first and develop courage to throw those ideas into Friday's whole-class conversations (Goal 8).

Much about the weekly routine helps students build successful habits, including the weekly draft deadlines. Students plan how to use their time in class to manage the deadlines effectively (Goal 9).

Navigating Obstacles 3.3

What if I'm required to follow a defined weekly or daily schedule?

Hopefully in this situation, a group of teachers is working together to make shared decisions about the schedule. But whether this is the case or not, push for clarity about what exactly is required of all teachers and where individual teachers have room and flexibility to make their own decisions about the schedule. I know I can't pull off what my colleagues down the hall can, and they don't go about things exactly the way I do either.

As an example, I tried Penny Kittle's daily routine for reading, writing, and revising. I just couldn't do it. Everything felt too rushed for me. I wanted bigger blocks of time for my students to work and more time to think about planning rather than having to plan for all of the pieces every day of class. But her schedule inspired me to think about how I could craft a regular routine that would work for me, my students, and my teaching context while still protecting time and space for the same important work.

My colleagues and I strive to work together despite the different ways we approach things. We craft a shared vision, respect each other's differences, and trust that we're all working toward the shared goals in our individual ways. The balance we have with each other takes frequent, intentional conversation. The more we know each other, the more we trust each other as teachers.

I make adjustments to the routine as needed depending on the week, but starting my planning with this schedule reminds me that I have only limited time with my students each week. I must use it to give my students time to do the work that aligns with the learning goals.

The weekly routine also changes some depending on the learning goals for each particular course. The goals I've been sharing so far to model this process are for a class that is primarily a writing class. We read a lot, but all of the texts we read are in support of students' writing—they provide mentor texts to study as writers and they give students ideas for what to write about. That's why you see so much of the weekly routine blocked out as time for writing.

I also teach AP Literature and Composition, which is primarily a reading course, and my learning goals for it are different. Students write a lot, but all of it is in service of the main goal of the course, reading literature for the purpose of being able to interpret it analytically. Hence, the weekly routine for that course blocks out more time for discussion of texts so students can do that interpretive work together (Figure 3.5). Much of the writing is timed, in-class writing because students need that practice for the AP exam. And there's one big chunk of reading time—most of

Monday (50 min)	Time to read (30–50 minutes, depending on the week)
	Varies, could be looking at student writing, preparing for discussions or writing later in the week, writer's notebook writing, or doing AP exam test-prep practice
Tuesday (50 min)	Discussion of reading (whole-class seminars or facilitated by students); begins with time for writing in notebooks to gather ideas for discussion
Wednesday/Thursday (90 min) (half of classes each day)	Grade book check-in and learning goal progress update (5 minutes)
	Discussion of reading *or* timed writing (the close analysis students will do on the AP Lit exam) followed by peer feedback and possibly taking a look at student writing on the doc cam
Friday (50 min)	Discussion of reading *or* unstructured time for writing (revision of timed writing or more extended writing tasks) and writing conferences

Figure 3.5 My weekly routine for AP Lit

class on Mondays—instead of the daily 10-minute reading block for my other class. The weekly routines for both courses have similar elements, but they have different structures and emphasis, depending on the learning goals specific to each course.

LEARNING GOALS FOR AP LIT

1. The student actually reads a diverse range of literature (novels, short fiction, plays, poetry, essays) because we are human beings and reading complex, imaginative works gives us practice in living a human life and imagining the experiences of others.

2. The student reads literature carefully to arrive at unique, individual interpretations, which takes creativity, sustained attention, and interaction with the text.

3. The student closely reads poetry and passages of fiction to uncover how language works to achieve meaning.

4. The student maintains a vibrant writer's notebook for writing informally and creatively to explore initial responses and emerging ideas about literature. It becomes a visible extension of the mind.

5. The student writes and revises extended pieces of writing to hone interpretations about literature, paying close attention to what makes good writing and revising earnestly in response to feedback.

6. The student writes timed essays to practice focused, clear thinking about complex texts.

7. The student uses talk and discussion opportunities in class to express and work through original thinking about literature.

8. The student hones effective student habits: meeting deadlines, following instructions, paying attention to details, managing digital tools and spaces effectively to keep track of work, and planning time to protect space to read and think in our distracted world.

9. The student is a positive community member: provides high-quality feedback to peers on their writing, participates earnestly in small-group and whole-group conversations, moves through our classroom spaces (physical and digital) with kindness.

10. The student practices effective self-reflection, self-evaluation, and metacognition. Students know what they already know, what they want and need to know, what they've learned, and how well they've learned it.

Whatever courses you teach, consider what sort of weekly or daily routine would best support your students to get the practice they need. Do your students need shorter blocks of time for writing, or blocks of time that are more structured? Perhaps a catch-and-release minilesson always planned in the middle of a block of writing time? Do they need more time for talking about reading, or routines to help them find books? It doesn't really matter how time is structured as long as it lines up with the learning goals for the course and it works for you and your students.

Also consider if there are ways you might find more time to spend on what really matters. Is there anything you're currently doing in your classroom (either a routine or a specific task) that doesn't align with your learning goals? Could you jettison it? It takes constant vigilance to resist cluttering up our precious class time. My advice is to throw it to the curb if it doesn't support the learning goals.

With a classroom orbiting around meaningful work that supports your learning goals, the next step is to think about the feedback students will need as they do this work. Chapter 4 shows you how to build a classroom community focused on feedback, enabling students to get the frequent feedback they need—sometimes from you, sometimes from each other, and sometimes even from themselves.

Interlude

Semester Grade Letter by Elena, Grade 12, AP English Literature and Composition

A Slightly Stressful Sunday

I take my pancakes off the griddle, stack them, smother them with butter and maple syrup, grab my book, and walk over to the dining room table. I sit down, take my first bite, and open the book. At 11:00 am on Sunday morning, two days before I'm supposed to be finished, I read the first line of Ken Kesey's *One Flew Over the Cuckoo's Nest.*

Elena's letter is a beautifully constructed story. Via the tale of one Sunday, she is able to describe the growth toward her three chosen goals.

Here she starts to discuss her first goal, to actually read all of the assigned books for AP Lit, books that you'll see Elena finds quite challenging.

As I speed through the book, and begin the reading comprehension check, I regret not having started sooner. Why didn't I start it as soon as we finished *Gatsby*, like some people in my class did? Why did I feel that I only needed a week to read the book? And why, when that week arrived, did I start another book? Nevermind that *Vicious*, by V.E. Schwab, was one of the coolest and most intriguing books I had read all year; I ought to have focused on the task at hand. Now I'm stuck with barely any time left, and the need to read and comprehend this book directly conflicting with my desire for a relaxing weekend and the math homework and college essays I have.

Not that I'm surprised. Despite being an avid reader, I've always had issues with completing assigned reading. Whilst I know that all the books are usually very good, and want to be reading higher level books such as these, I cannot usually bring myself to read the assigned reading. I had thought I had turned a corner when I finished *The Great Gatsby* ahead of time, but apparently not.

I leave *Cuckoo's Nest* after chapter 3 to go and do some of my chores in my room. I actively resist the pull of my shelf of YA novels. I don't have time for those now. Besides, one of my goals for the year is to read more challenging books than the ones currently sitting up on my bookshelf that have made up most of my high school life. So far, I haven't been doing so well. It's difficult to find the time and the willpower to read the books that aren't simple wish fulfillment, and require just as much brainpower for me to interpret as a difficult math assignment.

I get enough of my chores done to decide I deserve a coffee and reading break. I reheat some of the coffee left over from 2 hours ago, grab *Cuckoo's Nest* and my laptop, plop down into the large purple chair in the corner of my living room, and continue on my mission. Having finished classifying the characters as acutes or chronics, I move on to the chapter by chapter interpretation of the book. As the questions ask me, I am forced to think about the deeper meaning of sentences and passages, instead of merely reading the pages in an attempt to grasp the plot and characters. As I scan the words a second time, a bit slower, I begin to think deeply about the words I am reading and what they

What she has up on her laptop is the reading comprehension check for **Cuckoo's Nest** *that she mentioned earlier in her story. As described in Chapter 3, rather than a reading quiz for accountability purposes, it's a tool students use to help them comprehend a difficult text. Elena describes how the questions invite her to think about deeper meaning as she reads.*

Here, Elena discusses her second goal, to read to come to her own unique interpretations.

really mean. After a minute or so, I have a formulated idea as to why "It's the truth, even if it didn't happen," is an important sentence that reflects much of the meaning of the book, and possibly humanity. I hadn't started the semester this way. I could think deeply about the meaning within a book, but not how it applied to the world as a whole. I was astounded the first time I said something in class, and Doc Z had told me it was a theme statement. And now I'm beginning to form them with just a little bit of extra thought.

But now my break is over. It's time to revise my common application essay. I open the document. I've already responded to many of the comments Doc Z left when she read through my essay, but I still haven't decided for a couple places how I want to word things, or if I want to include a specific anecdote. In those places I keep the comments she left me open, as well as adding my own for later. But fixing these things

In this paragraph, Elena describes her work toward her third goal, revising thoroughly to improve her writing.

is not the purpose of today's revision. Today, I open to the page in my writer's notebook where I've recorded common problems in my writing, as well as my timed write revision document so I can access the grammar help links Doc Z added in her feedback. Today, I am going to comb my essay for grammatical and conventional errors. It's a slow going process, especially since my passive voice detection skills are weak. But my essay has improved, at least somewhat. I get up and stretch, before heading to the kitchen. It's time for me to pack lunch for the week.

Elena is nearing the end of the thorough revision task (described in Chapter 3). Since she's focusing now on conventions, that means she's polishing details after making more significant revisions.

Later that night I lay in bed and force myself through yet another chapter of *Cuckoo's Nest*. I'm considerably enjoying the book, and because of that, my reading speed had decreased significantly as I digest every word. Yet even with that, I still wish I was doing something else, reading something else. Today is an exception, but I'm not used to prioritizing my LA work over everything else, no matter how much I enjoy it. I accept that I won't be able to finish *Cuckoo's Nest* in time for the deadline, put the book on my nightstand, and turn off the lights. As I drift off to sleep, I know that if I continue on like I'm doing in LA I will deserve a B for this semester.

    —Elena

Elena selected a B, and I agreed. She had made some good progress toward her goals but has work yet to do, particularly in her first goal to actually read all of the books assigned for class.

Chapter Four

Create a Classroom Culture of Feedback

THE GRADING SYSTEM PROJECTS THE IMAGE OF THE EXHAUSTED English language arts teacher wielding a red pen over stacks and stacks of student papers, laboring for hours alone on what adds up to nothing more than postmortem reports. And because we need points to put in the grade book, students might write only the number of papers we have time to grade.

The learning goals I have for my classroom now require students to write far more than I am able to read and respond to alone. My students need feedback on their work, but I've learned it doesn't have to come from just me—there's a better way. We can teach students to provide helpful feedback to each other and even to themselves. We can build a classroom culture where students are itching to share their work with each other, craving feedback in the same way they have waited expectantly for points. This chapter will help you imagine these different possibilities as it invites you to do the following:

- Nurture a positive feedback culture.
- Teach students about feedback.
- Share the feedback load with your students.
- Work more efficiently when you give feedback.

Nurture a Positive Feedback Culture

Before we do anything else, we have to first make the humans in our rooms comfortable with each other. Although it *should* be less scary for students to have someone else look at their work in a classroom focused on feedback rather than evaluation, even when the end goal is not about how "good" or "bad" something is, students may find it intimidating for their classmates to look at their work. They need to know and trust each other and their teacher.

To move them in this direction, I first focus on making my students feel noticed and honored by me, their teacher. In their first homework assignment, I ask students to read my syllabus—which is in the form of a letter (see Online Resources 4.1 and 4.2 for examples). The letter outlines what they'll be doing in class and why I approach it that way. Students write me back and I respond, engaging in a brief one-on-one conversation about who they each are as students and humans. This assignment is magic. I begin to know how they think, how their brains work, and what's important to them. It goes a long way toward students feeling safe, connected, and valued in my class. After this first assignment, I continue making space for one-on-one conversation with my students via reading and writing conferences, and I focus on the little things that show I notice them: greeting them at the door, thanking them for coming to class as they leave, asking them about their lives beyond school.

Students need strong connections with each other, too, so I also help students feel at home in a small group on the very first day of class. The day one seating chart places three or four students alphabetically into pod groups, which also helps me learn their names quickly (another strategy that makes students feel valued). Each pod becomes a "response group" for feedback on writing, for responding to ideas about reading, and for turn-and-talk opportunities in class.

My favorite strategy for getting the groups to gel is to give them 5 minutes and send them out in the school to take a group selfie (a groupie?). I challenge them to find a location in the school that somehow lines up with what we were talking about in class that day (best place to get some reading done, the place that is most sonnet-like, the place that lines up with the text we just read, etc.). They post their photos to our Google Classroom space, and once everyone is back in class, we scroll through them and guess what the locations had to do with the task. Then I print the photos and put them on the wall behind each pod.

Another favorite connecting activity is to ask small groups to discover three things everyone in the group has in common (must be more interesting than "We all have eyes") and one thing that is unique to each person in the group. The conversation helps the group make connections, and when they share the results out to the class, we all learn a bit more about the people in the room.

Beyond these small-group tasks, I do quick group-building activities almost every day: "Turn to your pod and let them know how you're doing today," for example, or "There's a deadline coming up—turn to your pod and let them know what you need to take care of to meet the deadline." Even thirty seconds of this kind of conversation can forge connections between students, which is the ultimate goal if the groups will become good spaces for feedback.

Do not discount the power of a little silliness to forge group unity. I acquired a container of small, two-inch plastic dinosaurs recently and have started instigating occasional "dinosaur challenges." They go something like this: "I have a dinosaur for each person in the group that first shows me drafts in perfect MLA format." I had no idea small plastic dinosaurs would work so well to inspire students to help each other. And I'm talking about high school seniors here.

Finally, I think about ways to make my students feel overall class cohesion. Like me, you've probably had certain classes of students in the past that just gel. There's synergy. They all like each other. There is a peaceful calm about the room. You know that if for some reason you didn't show up, they would go ahead and run class themselves because they have all bought into the same overall purpose.

As a new teacher, I had visions of this kind of classroom energy but had no idea how to get there. Now I work toward it intentionally. For example, I take 5 minutes or so every day for the first week to do some whole-class icebreakers. There are so many ways to give students opportunities to talk to each other, to learn about each other, to make connections with each other, and to see the ways they are similar and different. Check out Liz Prather's *Project-Based Writing* (2017) for some of the best icebreakers I've seen, and hers are *also* idea-generating activities for writing.

Academic exercises like Socratic Seminars are also great for whole-class cohesion, and I use them frequently. My aim is for the conversation to feel like a family sitting around the dining room table talking about something that matters to them. I plan other opportunities for the whole class to focus on something together, even for a short time each day. Bonus if it's something that makes us laugh.

Helping students feel comfortable in your classroom does not need to take a lot of time, but it has a big impact on the classroom culture and is critical if students are to undertake the important job of managing the feedback load with you.

Teach Students About Feedback

For many of our students, response to their work means a grade when it's finished and comments to justify that grade. To these students, the whole idea of giving and receiving feedback that supports the process of their work will be new. They may wonder, "What do comments like this *sound* like? What's their intention? How do I know what to say?" To share the feedback load, we have to first teach students about the purpose and process of feedback and then continue to support their understandings about this thoughtful give-and-take across the year.

To start this conversation, I share with my students a list of five guidelines for giving feedback that I want them to use in their feedback to each other. I know it will take time and experience for them to really understand what these guidelines mean, but being explicit about them is an important first step.

1. *Feedback should help the student; the goal is not to improve the work.* We teach writers, not individual pieces of writing. We teach readers, not specific books. The best feedback focuses on the journey the human is on, not on the work itself: "The goal of feedback is to serve as a fulcrum for continued growth" (Ferriter and Cancellieri 2017, 2).

2. *Feedback should reflect—like a mirror—not evaluate.* Mirrors can only reflect what they see, like an observation. My colleague, Paul Bursiek, thinks of feedback as a mirror. By focusing on observations, we are more unbiased, whereas when we evaluate, our subjectivity comes into play, and we rely on opinion (Ferriter and Cancellieri 2017, 45). The best feedback observes and then reflects back what it sees.

3. *Feedback is a conversation.* As Maja Wilson explains, "In my view of feedback, every response constitutes an interaction between two human beings" (2018, 4). I love this—the conversation starts with a student's reading or writing or thinking and proceeds when someone else responds to it.

4. *Feedback should cause thinking* (Wiliam, quoted in Ferriter and Cancellieri 2017, 6). When feedback is a conversation, the resulting back-and-forth, person-to-person interaction is fertile ground for growth, leaving both humans with much to ponder.

5. *Feedback should tie to a student's learning goals* (Guskey and Bailey 2001, 104). Students set goals for reasons they find meaningful, so they are most receptive to feedback that will help them move closer to those goals. We also show respect when we work to help students achieve their goals.

Giving students some guidelines for feedback is a good way to start, but they also need ideas about what to say to provide helpful feedback. Absent that help, "Learners often slip into unhealthy patterns of using peer feedback as an opportunity to pass judgement on one another" (Ferriter and Cancellieri 2017, 45). Frameworks that offer different lenses for response and a variety of sentence stems to frame comments can help students become skilled at the kind of feedback these guidelines suggest. (See Figures 4.1 and 4.2.)

Figure 4.1 Students can use this framework as three steps to follow or as three different approaches to giving feedback (from Ted Nellen, as cited in Wilson [2006, 93–94]).

✳ **I heard** . . . As a reviewer, first try to summarize what you think the piece was about. This is the easy part. Tell the writer what you saw as the story or the main idea. As a writer, listen to this section, and try to hear whether or not you communicated what you were trying to communicate.

> *Stems such as "I heard" and "I noticed" invite students to reflect back to the writer what they see in their work, like a mirror.*

> *This guidance helps writers know what to do with the feedback they receive.*

✳ **I noticed** . . . As a reviewer, tell the author about some of the things that attracted your attention. What worked well? What details seemed especially vivid or striking? What will you remember about this paper? As a writer, think about why the reviewer noticed these things, and how you can make all your writing as effective.

✳ **I wondered** . . . As a reviewer, did you have any questions when you finished reading? Did you not understand what something meant, or why it was included? Did something bother or disturb you? Did you suspect something might have worked better another way? This is your chance to ask the writer all these questions. As a writer, try to answer the reviewer's questions. Look at your writing again, and see if there is any way to make those points clearer to the reader.

> *Posing questions to a writer begins a conversation with them.*

> *By answering the reviewer's questions, the writer continues the conversation.*

Figure 4.2 Feedback framework from Sara Donovan (2015) via middleweb.com

1. *Respond as a human being:* How does this text affect you emotionally or personally? What connections can you make to the topic personally in your life or in the life you hope to have?

> ✳ "Your essay/poem/critique resonated or spoke to me personally because _____."
>
> ✳ "I appreciate you writing on this topic because in my life _____."
>
> ✳ "This topic/idea hits me in the heart because I really care about _____."

> *The sentence stems for responding like a human being promote feedback that inspires thinking. Writers can think about the impact of their work on reviewers and whether or not that impact is what they intended.*

2. *Respond like a reader:* What did you learn? What will you do with this information? How have your beliefs or thinking on this shifted because you've read this essay?

> ✳ "I understand you better as a person because you've shared this story about _____."
>
> ✳ "I am grateful that you've trusted us with this experience about _____."
>
> ✳ "I never knew about this" or "I will try your suggestion because _____."
>
> ✳ "This is a fresh perspective on _____ because usually people talk about it like _____."
>
> ✳ "I understand the text/character/conflict/plot better now because before I thought _____ and now _____" or "I missed that part about _____ when I read _____."

> *Sentence stems like this put the focus on the writer more than on the work, enabling feedback to help the writer first.*

3. *Respond as a writer:* Which line or phrase seemed most vivid or funny or descriptive or unexpected but good?

> ✳ "The line that seemed most powerful/insightful in my view was _____ because _____.
>
> ✳ "The features of this genre that you did well were _____. For example, _____."
>
> ✳ "One technique I noticed was _____; for example, _____."
>
> ✳ "Something unique (fresh or surprising) that you did was _____."
>
> ✳ "The best example you gave was _____."

> *Here's the mirror again. The sentence stems for responding as a writer require the reviewer to reflect the work back to the writer.*

I copy these frameworks on one piece of paper that my students tape into their writer's notebooks. We talk through them briefly, and then they each highlight the perspectives, approaches, or sentence stems they want to use to provide feedback. You can also just choose one perspective, approach, or sentence stem and ask your students to use it on a particular feedback occasion. "Today, we're all going to respond like readers," for example. "Take a look at the sentence stems provided for responding like readers and choose one to guide your feedback."

I have also asked students for examples of feedback that *isn't* helpful. They've all gotten plenty of it and can usually name what doesn't work for them. Here are some common responses:

1. *Empty praise.* Students say a response such as "Good!" isn't helpful because it doesn't point out exactly what the reviewer thought was good.

2. *Anything mean.* Students say they don't want reviewers to be mean or call them stupid or laugh at something they are trying genuinely to accomplish. Mean isn't helpful.

3. *Sugarcoating.* Students say they want the honest truth. What's working and what's not?

4. *No suggestions.* Students say they want ideas from reviewers for what they could do to improve.

Finally, the purpose of feedback is to nudge readers and writers along on their journey of growth, so a shared vision of the end destination is critical. Students need to know, "What are we aiming for as readers and writers? Where is the feedback meant to take us?" To answer these questions, students need to see lots of examples of exemplary work—both professional and student mentor texts. They need to have conversations about the qualities of good reading and writing and to work together to name those qualities explicitly. In the next sections, I'll show you how I incorporate building this shared vision of quality work into the process of feedback itself.

Share the Feedback Load with Your Students

If students are reading and writing enough to grow, they need more feedback than a single teacher can give. So, whether it's a stack of timed writings, or reading responses, or writer's notebook tasks, or drafts of just about anything, I have a few strategies

I turn to again and again to enlist my students' help with the feedback load. The strategies are nimble enough to support readers and writers in lots of different ways, so they can be used across a wide range of tasks. They also expand the definition of feedback (beyond one person telling another what they think) to include any kind of work that helps a student reflect and revise.

SEVEN WAYS TO SHARE THE FEEDBACK LOAD WITH YOUR STUDENTS

1. Ask students to color-code their work and examine it for patterns to get ideas for revision.
2. Use a checklist or rubric to guide peer feedback in small groups or for student self-assessment.
3. Engage students in conversation with each other about their work.
4. Challenge students to find a mentor text that gives them ideas for revision.
5. Teach a minilesson to the whole class and ask students to reflect individually on how that minilesson applies to their own work.
6. Facilitate a peer feedback circle.
7. Choose the work of one student and have the whole class look at it together.

Color-Code a Draft

One way to help students think about their writing analytically is to have them color-code a draft to highlight different components. Color-coding is particularly helpful for writing argument. I provide a tub of colored highlighters and a coding key so the colors mean the same from student to student. (Students whose eyes can't distinguish color can use the key as a list of labels instead.) I ask students to highlight their thesis statements in pink, body paragraph claims in blue, data to support those claims in green, and warranting of the data in purple.

Even if we've only got 10 minutes in class, it's enough time for students to reread what they've written and think about it carefully with the frame I've provided via a color-coding key. As they work, a quick visual scan provides useful information. I can even see it from across the room—a paper with no green means the student either has no data to support claims or is not quite sure what data should look like, for example.

I throw out questions for students to consider: "Are you missing any of the colors? Does any one color seem to dominate? How different do the colors in your paper look from your neighbor's?" And always—"What do you think might be going on?" Almost immediately students begin articulating strategies for revision: "My data could be more specific," or "I couldn't find a claim in this paragraph," or "I don't have much purple. I need to work on developing my warranting more."

This simple strategy leads to feedback students can use to grow, and it also teaches them a way to provide feedback on their own without a reader or teacher. I have actually had students visit me after going to college admit that they continue to color-code their papers!

Use Checklists or Rubrics

As I've discussed in earlier chapters, when they're used to assign grades, I believe checklists and rubrics are extremely problematic. As tools, however, we can repurpose and use them as helpful guides for feedback. A checklist can help students zero in on key qualities of reading and writing.

After studying a variety of mentor texts in a particular genre, students (individually, in small groups, or even as the whole class) can make a checklist of the qualities of strong writing in the genre, then use the checklist to guide their own work and their feedback to each other. (See Figure 4.3.)

Genre Checklist, Commentary

▶ There is an obvious opinion.
▶ Put your thesis where it makes the most sense.
▶ Establish the issue early.
  ◆ Make sure the topic is one that other people may have differing opinions on.
▶ You have to have your own voice.
  ◆ Sound like you know what you're talking about (helps with your credibility).
  ◆ Use the right words to say what you want to say.
  ◆ Be concise.
▶ There are facts or some data or examples to support and validate your opinion.
  ◆ And you explain how those things do support/validate your opinion.
▶ Provide necessary background information.

Figure 4.3 A checklist my students made as we studied the argumentative genre of commentary

To develop this checklist, I used the classic think-pair-share. Students wrote silently about what they thought should be on the checklist, then shared that with their small groups, then the groups reported out to the whole class, and we built the checklist together. Each step required thoughtful reflection and conversation about the writing we had been studying and practicing. Students were then able to use the checklist to guide peer feedback and their own writing. The checklist itself was not the goal—the process to create it was the point.

If there's an existing rubric you like or are required to use, you can also use it as a helpful anchor for feedback. For example, the College Board provides the rubrics used to evaluate students' essays for the free response questions on the AP English Literature and Composition exam. I use these rubrics to acquaint students with how their writing will be evaluated on the AP exam and to help them develop a shared vision of what success looks like for this very particular writing task. In the past, I assigned grades to the rubric scores (5/6 = A, 4 = B, 3 = C, etc.), but I no longer do that. The rubric scores are simply data points along my students' learning journeys.

My students interact with rubrics in different ways. I sometimes ask them to work in groups to come to consensus on rubric scores for each of their timed writings (or for a stack of timed writings from another group). Or I might ask students to pair up with a buddy, read, and determine a rubric score for their classmate's paper and then discuss their reasoning for the score. I might ask students to determine a rubric score for their own paper and then do some writing to explain why they chose that score. The goal is for students to think carefully about the writing task, how well their writing or someone else's succeeded, and how the writing could be stronger—all without me having to spend a few hours going through the stack of papers on my own.

Engage in Conversation

Once you realize that any classroom conversation focused on what students think, have written, or have read is feedback, you'll see all sorts of ways to give students helpful, engaging feedback without taking any of your time outside of class. For example, you might ask students to explain to classmates what they wrote about and have the classmates report back what they heard, or have students talk in small groups about their plans for a certain task or to give an update about how their work is progressing. I even structure my seating chart to create opportunities for this kind of conversation. With every invitation I make for small-group conversation early in the school year, my hope is that eventually my students will turn to each other for conversation about their work without me asking them to.

Navigating Obstacles 4.1

What if I'm required to use a specific score-based rubric?

Rubric scores can provide valuable information, especially when collected over time so you can see trends in student work. Students can also examine the collected score data to evaluate their own learning (Chapter 7). But if recorded as a grade, the rubric score becomes high stakes, and students may focus more on the grade than the work. The solution? Use the score as just another data point but don't calculate it into a student's overall grade.

In addition to small-group talk, I sometimes put students in two concentric circles, lined up across from another classmate, and we engage in what I call "speed dating feedback." I give them thirty seconds to explain something they're working on or thinking about and then thirty seconds for the other student to respond. Then one of the circles rotates so each student gets a new talking partner and has the same conversation. We do this several times, and in the space of only a few minutes, students get significant feedback from peers.

Speed dating feedback is especially effective when my students are working on multigenre papers that challenge writers to think outside the box (Romano 2013, 4). My students sometimes struggle with this, so a well-timed speed dating feedback session lets them see how their classmates are approaching their writing and can help them imagine new possibilities.

I make sure everyone has their mostly complete first drafts in hand (either on paper or on a Chromebook), and the task is to walk their partner through the draft, pointing out the different genres they've used, explaining how they fit together. Then the partner responds. As students talk, I manage time to keep the activity moving and listen in on conversations to see what I can glean about where my students are struggling and succeeding with their drafts. At the end of the speed dating feedback session, I pull the class back together and ask a few students to share something they saw in a classmate's paper that was intriguing. I also ask students to make notes about any new possibilities they imagined in the process of sharing their drafts.

Study a Mentor Text

Writers seek out mentor texts all the time to help them figure out what they need to do with their own writing. When I officiated my cousin's wedding, for example, the first thing I did was look for examples of wedding ceremony scripts to get an idea of their components and characteristics. Studying mentor texts is a powerful way for writers to form a vision for their own work and to get feedback without needing a reader to respond. Ferriter and Cancellieri explain, students "compare their work against exemplars of success, and draw conclusions about next steps based on an understanding of their own strengths and weaknesses. The goal . . . is to give students opportunities to practice making decisions about what's next based on feedback that they gather on their own" (2017, 52).

Students will learn to seek out mentor texts and use them to guide their work if you show them how to do this. This means first looking at mentor texts together and pointing out the moves students can try out in their own work. In *Writing with Mentors* (2015), Marchetti and O'Dell offer a helpful framework for this that I use with my students:

* *Structure moves:* Focus on how the pieces of the text work together. For instance, does it have strictly or more loosely defined sections? How does it move from one paragraph to the next? Is there a clear lead and ending?

* *Ideas and detail moves:* Focus on the content of the piece, large and small. For instance, do unexpected details pop up in the writing? Are topics included that you had not previously considered?

* *Sentence moves:* Focus on the syntax, punctuation, and patterns that create striking sentences. For instance, does the writer use interesting syntax or repetition that you could mimic? Is there unique punctuation?

✱ *Word choice or tone moves:* For instance, does the writer use interesting word combinations? What in the writing signals the attitude of the writer toward the subject? How could it help you sharpen your own attitude in your writing? (78)

Rather than spending significant time providing feedback to students on a stack of papers, consider asking your students to find a mentor text to guide their work, then draw on other strategies to work with these texts. For example, if both are arguments, you might invite students to color-code for thesis, claims, data, and warranting in the mentor text and in their own writing and then compare and contrast the resulting visual information. How does each text use the same components of argument differently? What ideas does that present for revision? Invite students to have conversations about the mentor texts they found, explaining to a classmate or small group how the text is helping them to think about their own work. Or you might ask everyone in the class to isolate a specific kind of move—say, word choice—in their mentor text and share it with the whole group. The key is, by showing students *how* to use mentor texts to guide their own writing, we show them that they can work independently to improve it.

Teach a Minilesson

Several years ago in his session at the fall Colorado Language Arts Society conference, Mark Overmeyer encouraged teachers to read only deep enough into a stack of papers to find something to teach the whole class. Genius.

Responding to students' writing with a minilesson based on their collective needs has become a powerful form of feedback in my classroom. Recently, I had a stack of timed essays from my AP Lit students. I read through them all and left very brief, encouraging notes on each one, but I also took notes on a separate piece of paper about the trends emerging from their work. I looked over the trends and decided what I wanted to teach the whole class, then selected a few example sentences from students' papers to illustrate the lesson.

The next day, I returned my students' papers, went through the brief lesson, then asked them to review their own work with the lesson in mind and make notes about how they would revise. They talked about their revision ideas in small groups, then a few students shared out with the class. I saved time by not writing detailed feedback on each paper but still provided helpful feedback students could individualize for their own writing.

Facilitate a Peer Feedback Circle

Sitting together in a feedback circle, students bring drafts on paper with a note to readers to focus their feedback on the help the writer most needs. I give them 5–6 minutes per paper to read and respond, and then they pass the paper on to the next reader. Here are some examples of the kinds of feedback students have asked for in these circles:

- ✴ I need help finding a good way to end this piece.

- ✴ Where can I add deeper words with more meaning?

- ✴ I could use some help revising my sentences so they are not so wordy.

- ✴ I might add more so this may not be completely done yet. I just want to know if I should make it a little longer or just leave it as is.

- ✴ Should I put in more detail and dig further still into my thesis idea?

I sometimes pause between rounds of feedback and ask students to talk about something they've seen in a classmate's paper that they think is working well. At the end of the feedback circle, students will have read several papers and received feedback from several readers—two benefits of this activity. I always leave at least 5 minutes at the end of the circle for students to read the feedback they received on their drafts—they are usually anxious to do this.

Feedback circles can be digital as well. On one shared Google Doc, I list students' names and they put a link to their paper next to their name. Starting with the paper of the student listed right below their name, students read and offer feedback, continuing on down the list. When they get to the bottom of the list, the next paper to read and respond to is the one by the student at the top of the list. This simple process ensures that students are giving and receiving feedback evenly across the class.

I like to participate in feedback circles with my own drafts as well (Figure 4.4). This gives me the chance to read and respond to a few students' papers during the activity, and it also says to my students that the work I've assigned them is important enough that I'm doing it, too. (I can't always accomplish this, but I write with them whenever I can.)

Either digitally or on paper, a feedback circle can lead to extensive feedback for each student, all done in class, all without time spent by the teacher outside of class.

Figure 4.4 Student feedback on my rough draft literary analysis about *Slaughterhouse Five*

Questions for my readers: What I have here is my intro and a rough plan for the rest of the essay. Please think about the following as you read: Have I made a strong case that Billy is NOT time traveling? Any details I need to include? Does the progression of the claims make sense? Any additional claims I need to establish to make my argument?

> the examples from the book feel like solid details to support your claims.

> yes, but the first claim seems more subjective than the others.

> the claims seemed stronger as they went.

> I think all the ideas you need are here but maybe not in the best order yet.

There is no question that war is traumatic. I've read umpteen books about the horrible moments of war (*Matterhorn, All the Light We Cannot See, The History of Love, Sarah's Key, The Things They Carried*). These books communicate the human consequences of war by telling stories of people involved in war or affected by it. Kurt Vonnegut's *Slaughterhouse Five* belongs in this group, but this book's focus is unique. It goes beyond stating simply that war is traumatic; the book takes on the question of how a person who experiences the death and destruction of war might manage the resulting memories for the rest of his life. Through the example of Billy Pilgrim and the author persona that bookends the text in the opening and closing chapters, the text argues that some trauma can be so extreme that the mind must create an alternate universe in order to mitigate the traumatic memories.

Points I want to make:

Billy is not actually time traveling. Vonnegut hints at this on p. 23.

Brain surgery as a result of a tragic plane crash is the traumatic event that brings on Billy's hallucinations of time travel. (use moment that shows Billy never discusses his supposed time traveling until later in his life and after the brain surgery p. 25).

The book offers clear clues to explain how Billy comes up with his story about being unstuck in time. (The moments surrounding the plane crash and its aftermath are spread throughout the text—first mentioned on page 25, continued on page 157, and concluded on pages 198-207 when Billy goes to New York City and tells his story live on a radio show—all after the war. But focus on the bookstore visit and the clues it offers that Billy is not actually time traveling p. 201-204.)

> the comparison between the books Billy sees in the bookstore and how they connect to his overall story works really well.

Figure 4.4 *Continued*

So if he's not time traveling, what is actually happening? He escapes traumatic memories by time traveling in his mind away from them. (use the moment when he escapes the delousing episode as a POW by time traveling to his childhood)

We cannot consider Billy's plight without considering Vonnegut's. This book is Vonnegut's response to the horrors he experienced. Like Billy, Vonnegut is plagued by traumatic memories. His memories are woven together with Billy's. (mention the moments when Vonnegut says that was me, I was there . . . the mustard gas and roses smell that shows up in many places in the text, the feet all over the text that are described as blue, the time when Billy gets a drunk dialed phone call—deliberate inclusion of the author persona in the narrative about Billy. Vonnegut cannot separate himself from this story. It is his story too.)

So this is Vonnegut's response to war . . . what does it tell us to do with this kind of trauma? As a Tralfamadorian novel? Focus on the beautiful moments, no one is ever really dead (so it goes).

Conclusion: Look back at intro and make sure it captures what I actually wrote about.

> also, maybe focus on whether it's the author's goal or not to make you think Billy is not actually time traveling.

> if uncertain what stance to go on regarding Billy's time traveling, discuss both? is the author trying to trick us into thinking Billy is time traveling?

> when the author jumps into it, it makes it seem like it's not real—the author jumping in is a link to reality—the author never shows up when Billy is in space . . . author jumping in as witness of the real things that happened.

> use so it goes more.

> w/ so it goes—death is so traumatic to him, can't escape to past and future and just stops it there with so it goes.

> focus here on what you think is most important to say. is it something about what the book is saying about dealing with trauma?

> maybe focus more on the idea of escaping trauma.

Look at an Example of Student Writing

Looking at strong student writing—even just a sentence or two—is another way to help students build a shared vision of quality work, and this writing often feels more accessible than mentor texts written by professional writers (which can seem out of reach). If my students are struggling with thesis statements, for example, we might look at one or two I've pulled from their papers and talk about why they're strong examples or how to improve them if that's what they need. If my students are struggling with wordiness, we might look at one or two wordy sentences together and think about how to make them more concise. Then students take what they've learned and use it to evaluate their own drafts for revision.

On occasion, I persuade a student or two to let me put an entire draft up on the big screen for the whole class to read and respond to. The prospect of this can be terrifying, so I never force a student to do this. But I usually get volunteers, especially if I ask a few days ahead of time.

Once we've got a student's work in front of us, I start by asking the writer two key questions:

* Is there is anything you want us to know about the piece before we read it?
* How we can help with our feedback?

These questions let the writer focus us as we read the piece so we can provide the feedback most needed. The writer (or I or another student) reads the draft aloud, then the students report out what they think is working in the writing. Next, we address the feedback the writer asked for and make suggestions guided by that focus. I make sure someone is taking notes, either the writer or someone in the writer's response group, so the writer can just focus on the conversation.

This activity provides extensive feedback to the writer, of course, but there are benefits for everyone else in the class, too. I ask students to reflect on what came up in the conversation that applies to their own work, and then to write this down, talk about it in small groups, or even report out to the class briefly if there is time.

Work More Efficiently When You Give Feedback

There are times, of course, when feedback needs to come from the teacher. I challenge myself to work smarter, not harder, at this so it doesn't take over too much of my time beyond school. Although this continues to be a work in progress for me, I find that each year I get a little better at three actions that make a big difference. To work more efficiently, I do the following:

* Find a focus for written feedback.
* Manage the paper load.
* Approach conferences with intention and organization.

Find a Focus for Written Feedback

Over time, I have learned to narrow my focus for written feedback. If I don't think about it, I'll mark pretty much everything in a piece of writing that a student could work on, which takes more time than necessary and overwhelms my students. First, I remind myself to think about what's most important for a particular writer to do and offer feedback on improving that. My students' chosen learning goals (more about this in Chapter 6), their writer's memos, and any checklists we've developed together help me to determine what's most important for a particular piece of writing and narrow my feedback.

Next, I think about what work students do that *needs* written feedback from me, and I carefully clarify the purpose of that feedback so my intentions are clear. There are four general categories of written work my students do that need my feedback: drafts, work in revision, published work, and reflections (Figure 4.5).

Out of these four categories of student work, providing written feedback on revision takes the most time because of my focus on individualized instruction. Responding to the other work goes fairly quickly. Even though my students may turn in drafts every week, I can get through one class' weekly drafts in an hour or less if I'm reading for the reasons I've outlined here. I can accomplish this the same day students turn in the drafts, sometimes even in my prep time at school before going home.

Manage the Paper Load

I don't know about you, but when I'm staring down a huge stack of papers I know will take me significant time to read and respond to, I can't even start with the first one. It's taken me over two decades of teaching to really figure this out, but it is *my* fault if I have an unmanageable tower of student work to get through. I am in control of when my students turn in their work, but to avoid the mountain of papers, I have to act with intention.

Drafts	I look at drafts to see how things are going, to determine next instructional moves, to figure out which students I will target with conferences, to show students I'm paying attention to their work, to get a baseline for where my students are starting. *I leave brief written feedback to encourage students and let them know I was there.*
Work in Revision	I look at work in revision to determine next instructional moves, to help students with what to focus on next, and to figure out which students need conferences. *I leave detailed written feedback because the task requires students to use it and keep working. I provide individualized instruction to help students grow and move forward.*
Published Work	I look at published work to determine next steps in the class and to get a sense of where my students have ended up. *I leave very little written feedback (sometimes none) because I am not the audience for their published work. Any written feedback is to celebrate their efforts and to help students see what they've learned and where they've grown.*
Reflections	I look at reflections to monitor progress, to see where students need support, to identify students for conferences, and to determine instructional moves. *I provide brief written feedback as needed to encourage and guide students and to help them see what they've learned and where they've grown.*

Figure 4.5 The purpose of feedback for each kind of work and the type of response I write

Rethink deadlines

I don't want to feel the weight of student work to respond to over the weekend, so I don't collect it on Fridays. I set no deadlines for Saturdays or Sundays, either, which online learning management systems make possible. If it's good for me to have weekends free of school work, it's good for my students too. I avoid Monday deadlines when I can for this reason, too.

Another thing I want my students to do is sleep. Hence, no 11:59 P.M. deadlines. I won't be looking at the work at midnight, so why would I ask for it then? Yes, of course students could work ahead of time and get the work turned in earlier, but I'm not helping them by setting a deadline when they should be sleeping. So, I set most deadlines for the days I plan to read and respond to the work, at the end of class or the end of school on a particular day when I can also provide time in class for students to work. I schedule due dates that help me to manage the work without feeling overwhelmed by it.

Be flexible

There's no reason why I can't also be flexible with deadlines. Sometimes my life blows up unexpectedly, and I know I won't be able to get to a stack of student work when I planned to, so I move the deadline to a time when I can read and respond to it. This keeps the work from stacking up and stressing me out. My students need flexibility, too, and I negotiate extensions with individuals as needed. They have to communicate with me about the time they need to do the work well. They have to think about the demands on their time and plan for when they will be able to get the work done. We'll set a new due date, which I record in the grade book so we both remember what it is, and students usually meet it.

So many of our students are managing more in their hours outside of school than we might realize. They might need to work multiple hours to help their families financially. They might have responsibilities for caring for younger family members. They might have activities after school that cut into their evenings. The least I can do is be flexible enough to account for the realities my students are juggling as I'm working to make my work life more manageable for me.

Stagger turn-in times

With some planning ahead, I can also avoid collecting work from multiple classes of students on the same day. When I assign something that I know will take significant time for me to respond to, I create a schedule over the course of several weeks for students to turn in the work. If two classes are doing a revision task, for instance, getting sixty papers at once will immobilize me, but I know I can handle about six per day. So, I make a schedule with slots for students to sign up for the due dates they want, and over the course of a few weeks, I make my way through them all. Because I know I can read and respond to the papers I get each day, the work is manageable and I remain caught up with it, which feels fantastic! Students get my feedback while their experience of doing the work is still fresh in their minds. And because students choose a due date that works for them, they have more flexibility.

Use technology

Google Docs is the best tool for teaching writing I have ever used, with features that help me work as efficiently as possible when I review my students' revision work. I have them revise in suggesting mode, which reveals their revision work immediately so I can quickly zero in on the changes they've made and offer feedback on how the revisions are working. I also ask them to never resolve the comments I leave each time I look at their writing. Those comments help me to remember the conversation the student and I were having when I come back to a paper after the student has done more revision.

Reduce marginal notes

By default, I always wrote my comments in the margins of students' work, but I've learned to do less of that. When I offer feedback in the margins, students often simply make changes at each comment without thinking about the piece of writing as a whole. If I offer, instead, a paragraph of feedback at the end of the paper, they have to read my response and ponder where and how they want to address it in revision.

To help me focus this end-of-paper feedback, I've made a table that I copy and paste into the student's document and then record my notes (see Figure 4.6). Notice that students fill in the last box in the table, and this creates a cycle of revision and

Stuff to think about as you revise	
Mechanics to review—look for these errors to fix	
Doc Z's experience reading	
Doc Z's response to your revision memo	
AFTER YOU REVISE, write an updated memo here explaining which parts of my feedback you used and how you used it.	

Figure 4.6 Feedback table

feedback, as I respond to this memo each time I look at the evolving draft. I have found that it actually takes me less time to do this kind of written feedback than it took me to evaluate students' work for grades on rubrics. Free of the need to evaluate, and free of having to justify any points I take off, I can simply respond to what I see, describing it so the students can use my reflective comments to monitor their own learning progress.

Approach Conferences with Intention and Organization

Like many of my teaching mentors, my strategy for a reading or writing conference is simple: get the student talking, listen, figure out what I can teach, then teach it. Briefly. I sit down beside students as they're working and ask, "How can I help you?" or "What are you working on?" or "How is it going?" Sometimes I need to pose a few more questions to get students talking, but mostly I listen until I get a sense of how I can help them move forward. To help me focus the conversation and teach with intention, I keep a chart in my writer's notebook showing each student's chosen learning goals.

When it comes to working more efficiently, one of the challenges of conferences is managing my notes on the conversations. At one point, I had a Google Form that I filled out after each conference and then copied and pasted the notes into my electronic grade book. I figured I could cut out a step if I just wrote the notes in my electronic grade book to begin with, so I did that for a while. But then I noticed that I didn't like having to carry my computer around the room and as a result, I was avoiding conferences. This was a problem, so I grabbed one of the fits-in-your-palm reporter's notebooks my journalism students use and started jotting down notes in it. Later in the day I would transfer my scribbles into notes in the electronic grade book. But then I stopped wanting to do that transcription, and that also got in the way of doing conferences.

Now I've gone back to a Google Form—this time for students to fill out after a conference conversation. They note what we talked about and what their next steps are in their work. I can quickly copy and paste these notes into the electronic grade book and easily review the conversations I have with students each day. This works pretty well, except for having to constantly remind students to fill out the form—I have plenty of conversations that never get recorded. The bottom line? I haven't found a perfect system, and it's a constant struggle to capture the instruction I do in conferences. But the notes are important for two reasons: (1) they will help my students to see the journey they have followed as learners, and (2) they inform my instruction. So I keep working to find a system that works.

Another challenge is making enough time for conferences. I do many of my conferences on the fly with students as they are reading or writing, sitting down to talk with them as they need my help. The problem is, this leaves out the students who don't seek my assistance, so on some days I make it my goal to get around the entire room for a brief conversation with each student. I ask something simple, such as "Tell me what you're working on today," and this gives me the chance to hear from them all and to monitor the progress of the whole group. At other times I ask every student in a class to sign up for a conference with me over the course of a week or so—there's something special about time reserved specifically for each student. It says, "You matter, your work matters, I'm reserving time for *you*."

When you carefully create a classroom culture of feedback, students get the response they need to grow as readers and writers, and you are able to manage the feedback load as a healthy, happy human being. The next step is to think about how you and—more importantly—your students will know they are learning, where you'll look for evidence of that learning, and what data you'll collect to reflect that learning. In Chapter 5 I'll show you how to use your electronic grade book to provide this important assessment data to your students so they can be the experts on their own learning.

Interlude

Semester Grade Letter by Kalliyan, Grade 12, AP English Literature and Composition

Dear Doc Z,

In January I walked into class with such high hopes that I would be an even better student than before. I even wrote it in my last letter. But that didn't happen. I became a worse student. A lazier student. I have become a student who barely makes due dates and that is not the student I want to be.

Kalliyan's brutal honesty here is not uncommon in my students' stories.

Although I have not been the responsible student I was supposed to be when it came to due dates, I made sure I was the responsible student when it came to my table mates. Although I tend to not be able to be there for myself, I make sure that I am the best teammate that I can be and that I other students can depend on me.

Kalliyan admits that her individual work was not stellar. But the classroom community—particularly the small group she sat with at her table each day— inspired some significant growth in her as a reader, which is what she mostly focuses on in her story.

At the beginning of the semester we were talking about *12th Night* by Shakespeare. My group and I were able to talk about the importance of sexuality and gender roles in the book when we see Viola pretend to be her brother in a time where men and women were clearly not seen as equal. The latest book that we have read was *Beloved*. I liked *Beloved* more with the complexity of the book and how challenging it was to read. I was really excited to talk about this book with my group and I thought that I could actually bring something relatively valuable to the table when we discussed about this book. When Doc Z had a class discussion about the impact of motherhood due to slavery she asked us if Sethe was either guilty or innocent when it came to the murder of her child. When we came to this discussion we came to the conclusion that she was guilty. But I thought that we are looking at it from a different time period and although we were trying to look at Sethe's actions from her point of view, we simply couldn't because none of us came close to even knowing what Sethe went through. Before reading this book, I took the time to become a better student. When I was confused I did not just try to move on, I actually reread the chapter then read the summary online to clear my confusion. I took the time to jot down what popped out to me in my writer's notebook. When we came back to school,

I was able to share my own original thoughts and I felt that I had brought something different and interesting about the book. I told my group mates about the significance of red and when Doc Z over heard it and also agreed it made me feel like my work was worth its while this time.

This semester I started reading more philosophical books and in doing so it has opened my eyes to think differently and look at life and even justice in this matter differently and less straightforward. The books that I have chosen to read on my own are books I have never even thought about picking up and now I am reading (or at least trying to read) Plato. I am pushing myself like never before and I am becoming better for it.

The literature that we have read this year forced me to look at topics from a different angle and the books made me learn how to get out of my comfort zone and interpret things in a new light. I have had adult conversations about adult topics like politics with my father and I strongly believe that this class has helped me with it. I have noticed that I have become more confident as an individual. I started to talk more in my classes and I put forward more in conversations that I had in group discussions and class discussions.

In setting the goals that I did, I have forced myself to read more books in order to reach my goal. At first it was quite difficult, but then I noticed that I was eventually reading for the betterment of myself. I knew I had finally reached my goal when I started picking up my book rather than my phone and I believe that that was my biggest accomplishment this year. I do still need to work on comprehending while I am reading and I do still need to focus on not zoning out while I read, but I have come farther than I would have expected.

I would like a C for the end of this semester. I completed my goals and ended where I wanted to end as a person (for now), and although I could have done a lot better as a student, I am happy with where I ended as a student as well. I should have been more on top of my assignments, but I think overall I learned more and I grew more this year than any other year. I finally found books that I can read without getting bored and through these books I have finally found something more to my life. This year has taught me to look past just the cover of things and I have become a better person for it. Before all I thought that I had was my social media, some games and nail polish. Now I have Freud, and Plato and Eckhart Tolle. When people ask me what I like to

Kalliyan selected a C for the semester, and I agreed. Though she achieved significant growth in her goals for reading, she opted not to fully complete some of the most important work for the class, leaving only a partial view of the growth she could have achieved.

do on my free time I can say that I read. Now I can talk about the psychodynamics of our inner selves or the spirituality that we hold through Plato and Socrates. I am beyond happy with where I am now, and I am excited to see what I learn next.

—Kalliyan

Given a points-based approach, the numbers probably would have added up to a C as well, but missing would have been this extensive story about how Kalliyan became a reader. Because she wrote it, I can see her more clearly than a collection of points would allow. But more importantly, Kalliyan now knows exactly what she learned and how she learned it.

Chapter Five

Make the Learning Visible

YOU MAY REMEMBER THAT IN CHAPTER 1 WE LOOKED AT AN EXAMPLE of typical points-based grade book data for a student's work over a few weeks, and we acknowledged that this data doesn't tell us much about the student's learning journey (Figure 5.1). In contrast, words-based grade book data (Figure 5.2) reveals a much clearer, richer portrait of that student's journey.

Assignment	Points possible	Points earned	Score
Song/video analysis argument draft	20	16	80.0
Advertisement analysis argument draft	20	17	85.0
Satire analysis argument draft	20	12	60.0
A Place to Stand analysis argument draft	20	18	90.0
Revision of an analysis argument	50	47	94.0
OVERALL GRADE	**130**	**110**	**84.6**

Figure 5.1 Points-based grade book data

Assignment	Comments
Song/video analysis argument draft	You analyzed the song "Chop Suey." You talked about how the song dealt with the topic of suicide. Warranting could be more developed, and think about having a dedicated concluding paragraph.
Advertisement analysis argument draft	You wrote an analysis of the Gillette ad. You argued that despite the ad's good intentions, it didn't work very well. Work on identifying the claims more precisely. Warranting is more developed than the song analysis. There's no separate concluding paragraph.
Satire analysis argument draft	We extended your deadline by a few hours because you said you were having a hard time focusing on your ideas in class. You analyzed the *Saturday Night Live* Alexa skit. You have a good start—you didn't get much written today. But there's lots to build on here if you choose to revise.
A Place to Stand analysis argument draft	You wrote about how Jimmy didn't have much choice about his actions. The color-coding shows good understanding of claim/data/warranting. There's no separate concluding paragraph.
Revision of an analysis argument	You revised your *A Place to Stand* analysis, adding to it (including a conclusion) and reworking several sentences. Your peer reader suggested adding more specific data to support your claims. You did this.

Figure 5.2 Words-based grade book data

Words-based data are descriptive, not evaluative, and these words reflect back to the student, Cassie, the work she has been doing. She can see growth—a note to focus on warranting in the first paper and a description that she did that for the second paper. She can see that she continually omitted conclusions on her analyses but eventually conquered that in her revised piece. We have more information about that third paper. There's a description indicating that Cassie was having a difficult time focusing on the writing that day. Even the extended time didn't enable her to get a lot written. Whatever was distracting her with that paper, it was clearly a blip when you see this collection of descriptive data about her work across these tasks. In a points-based system, that one blip might cost her a letter grade. Here, it's useful information for her and for me. It's something we can talk about in a writing conference. It's something she can think about as she reflects on her journey as a learner for the semester.

Not surprisingly, we can see Cassie in this words-based data far better than we can see her in the numerical scores, an idea Tom Newkirk explores in *Minds Made for Stories* (2014). Statistical data, Tom explains, are not as persuasive to us as we might think: "We have an ambivalent attitude toward hard statistical data; our rational side tells us that this kind of evidence should be conclusive and should trump anecdotal accounts that may well be unrepresentative, and, given the fallibility of human memory, not all that accurate. Yet we are rarely persuaded by numerical data alone" (109). He sees a critical problem in schools where "teachers are now coached to rely on 'data'" in the form of test scores; we just cannot find our students in the numbers (110).

Words-based data do more than help us see our students more clearly; they also help us know better how to teach them, a point Rick Stiggins explains in *The Perfect Assessment System* (2017):

> In the classroom context, grades and test scores do not convey the diagnostic information that can help teachers pinpoint and address student strengths or weaknesses, nor do they provide teachers with anything substantive to pass on to students in order to enhance their understanding of how to achieve success or help them engage in self-assessment. . . . Students need continuous access to descriptive feedback that describes their work and informs them about how to do better next time. Given this feedback, they will be able to track and understand changes in their own academic capabilities over time. (79–80)

We already offer our students lots of feedback through our notes on their writing and the conferences we have with them, but our grade books can provide students with "continuous access to descriptive feedback that describes their work" (Stiggins 2017, 79). If we collect descriptive statements of students' work—in words—they will have the information they need to see *for themselves* what they are learning and where they need to redirect their efforts. Learning to reflect on their work independently helps students continue to grow as readers and writers beyond our classroom walls. Research supports this. John Hattie's *Visible Learning* (2008) meta-analysis of hundreds of research studies in education shows that student self-reported grades have one of the strongest impacts on student achievement. But students need the right kind of information that provides a clear picture of the work they are doing.

And finally, words-based data provide helpful information to other data users of the grade book as well. Students' parents, special education teachers, English language development (ELD) teachers, and any other teachers who might work with them can see exactly what they are learning and working on and can use that information to support them. So rather than amassing a collection of points in your grade book, this chapter will show you how to build portraits of students as learners, word by word, by inviting you to do the following:

- Think of your grade book as a data warehouse.
- Determine what data you actually need to see your students' progress toward the learning goals.
- Take control of the math machine in your grade book.
- Imagine what you could do with your grade book by considering some grade book examples.

Think of Your Grade Book as a Data Warehouse

The numbers-based electronic grade books required of many of us take some critical decisions away from us about assessment. Whether the grade book is based on percentages or some kind of standards-based scale, it assumes that we will enter a number for every single task we record, a number that goes into the math machine and calculates an ongoing overall grade. But what if the numbers aren't the information we need?

From the world of computing comes the concept of the data warehouse—a system for pulling together multiple data sources into one central location, accessible for multiple users who can look across the data to assist in decision-making. Data warehouse designers consider which data to include, who might use the data and how, and what kinds of reports and analyses will come from the data and for what purposes.

Thinking about your grade book as a data warehouse rather than a place to collect points opens up new possibilities for supporting readers and writers. Most online grade books required by schools or districts are data management systems that track scheduling, attendance, discipline, and grades. Multiple users can view the grade book: students, parents, administrators, counselors, other teachers, school support staff (Figure 5.3). This reporting tool is already a powerful platform to become a data warehouse, so to make the shift, the first step is to think about designing a robust collection of data. You will need data you can use to inform your instruction for your students both collectively and individually. You'll also think about the information your students and any other grade book users need and how the grade book will broadcast that information so it's most usable for all parties.

Notice I've not included any questions about grades. Yes, a student might wonder, "What grade do I have?" and many who are used to seeing only numbers

Grade book users	Data needs
Students	Am I keeping up with my work? What did the teacher and I discuss in our conference last week? What do I need to work on? What am I learning?
Classroom teacher	Which of my students are not keeping up with the work? Where are my students struggling? Who should be on my conference list today? And what should we talk about? What did I talk about in my last conference with that student?
Parents	Is my child keeping up with the work? What is my child learning? What does my child need to work on? What is my child working on in this class? How can I support my child's learning at home?
Special education teachers **ELD teachers** **Study hall teachers**	Is the student keeping up with the work? Where is the student struggling? What conversations has the teacher had with the student about the work? What does the student need to do next?
School counselors	Is the student keeping up with the work? Is the student on track to graduate? Where is the student struggling?
School administrators	Which students are eligible this week for athletic participation? How many students are struggling? Are students all on track to graduate? What are the students' progress report grades?

Figure 5.3 Grade book users and their data needs

in grade books *will* wonder this, at least at first. But the numerical answer to that question does not show the student what she's learned, or what she and the teacher talked about in a conference, or what she needs to work on to grow. You and your students can become partners in shifting their focus to learning instead of points if you invite them into dialogue with you. Ask them about their experiences with grades and learning in school, and really listen to them. If students know *why* you aren't grading as usual and *how* it can help them, they can take a different stance toward the work in your class—they can do the work for themselves, to learn, rather than to collect points.

Navigating Obstacles 5.1

What if it seems your students' parents want grades?

Guskey and Bailey (2001) explain, "The vast majority of parents say they would like to receive more detailed information about how their child is doing in school" (21). I have found this to be true. Parents want more detailed information about their students and are happy to get behind a system that provides more than what they have received in the form of grades in the past. For example, they know that a low grade indicates some struggle, but words tell them what the struggle is, which is so much more helpful.

Back-to-school night is an excellent place to address this issue with parents. You can explain how the grading system impedes learning and that you're doing what you can to work around that. Make sure parents know how to interpret what they'll see in your grade book, how final grades will be determined, and how they can support their student from home.

For parents who do not make it to back-to-school night, make information available in other ways—posted on your school webpage, emailed out to parents, sent home in a letter—whatever it takes to help them understand. In the Online Resource 5.1, you can see the information about my approach to grading that I publish on my website for parents and students.

Even so, some parents can be uncertain. Assure them that you're happy to look over the assessment data with their child at any time and talk about how it's going.

Determine What Data You Need

The next step is to determine what kind of data you actually need to help you see evidence of students' learning. For each of your learning goals, you will need to consider these questions:

- ✷ What does it look like if my students are progressing toward this goal? What will I see?

- ✷ Where can I look for their learning in the work I assign?

- ✷ What data will I collect in my grade book to show this learning?

As an example, let's consider the learning goal "The student is a reader with a vibrant, self-directed reading practice that will continue beyond my classroom." I will know that students are growing toward this goal if they read more books than they initially thought possible. Maybe I'll even see them creating lists of books to read in the future (as Penny Kittle says in *Book Love* [2012], readers have plans). I will see students reading books that matter to them, and reading regularly, carving out the time each week necessary to build a practice.

The work I have planned for my students to do toward this goal should show evidence of their growth: the weekly reading check-in Google Form responses, reading conferences (individual and group), observations of students' daily silent reading, and any writer's notebook pages connected to their reading progress. But what will I record in the grade book? What data would be helpful to look at across a few weeks that might show growth? What data will help my students determine for themselves where they have grown and where they still need to grow? Thinking about it in this way, I designed my weekly reading check-in Google Form to include a few simple questions that reveal progress toward this learning goal. Students fill it out once per week:

1. How much time did you spend reading in the past week? (Two to three hours is the goal.)

2. What did you read?

3. How did the reading go for you? Please include whatever got in the way of reading if it did. Also include how the reading is helping you with your writing for class.

4. What will you read in the next week and when do you plan to read it?

With a simple copy and paste of students' responses into the comment fields in my grade book, I can collect an entire class' responses in under 5 minutes. This gives me excellent data on each student that, over several weeks, construct a detailed portrait of students as readers—what they're reading, how much time they're spending, how the reading is influencing their other work for class, and anywhere they are struggling.

Better than a collection of points, this is information I can act on as a teacher. I can see immediately which students I should reach out to with a conference—either to offer some support or to celebrate an accomplishment. And it reflects back to students the work they are doing; they can use it to evaluate their learning. Figure 5.4 shows Noah's weekly reading check-in responses over a few weeks.

Date	Comments entered into weekly reading check-in Google Form
2/16	1 hour: *Cuckoo's Nest*, *Dying for a Living*. I was out of state for most of the week last week and didn't have very much time to read. Just keep reading as much as I can.
2/23	1 hour: *Cuckoo's Nest*, *Dying for a Living*. Didn't meet the goal because I've been super busy, haven't been home, hard to focus on anything after school all day. I'll keep reading as much as I can, more with *Cuckoo's Nest* to make sure it's easier to stay up to date.
3/2	Less than 1 hour: *Cuckoo's Nest*. There's been so much going on that I haven't been able to read. I'm not able to balance everything else and reading very effectively. I will keep reading as much as I possibly can.
3/9	I almost finished *Cuckoo's Nest* by today's book group conversation.
3/16	1.5 hours: "Eyes of Wood," "Heart of Stone," "The Ghost in Angelica." I think it's easier to read many shorter things than one long story. So that's good for me at least. That also makes it easier to read for the full time too.
4/2	2 hours: *13 Reasons Why*, *Dying for a Living*. Both books are pretty good. Not super far into *13 Reasons*, but it's good so far. *Dying for a Living* got to an intense spot.

Figure 5.4 Noah's weekly reading check-in responses over a few weeks

When Noah looks back over this information, he will see how his reading progressed from struggling with *One Flew Over the Cuckoo's Nest* to finding more time for the shorter texts and books he chose on his own in later weeks. What could he learn about himself as a reader by reflecting on this? He reports struggling to find time to read *Cuckoo's Nest*, but I would ask him to consider if there was something about that book that made it more difficult for him to pick up and read. This would make an excellent focus for a reading conference, as would several other things I notice in this collection of data. For example, I might ask Noah:

- about his strategies for making time to read

- to tell me more about the intense spot in *Dying for a Living*

- if he watched the TV series for *13 Reasons Why* and what he thinks about how well that series interpreted the book

- to compare *13 Reasons Why* with *Dying for a Living*

- why he omitted his hours read for the week of March 9th

- if he needs more support during his reading of *Cuckoo's Nest*—what seems interesting or confusing so far? Let's talk about that!

The weekly reading check-in collects important data about my students' progress toward building a regular reading practice. Copying students' responses into the grade book pulls the information together in a format that makes it easy for my students and me to see. Students can use it to make decisions about their next steps as learners, and I can use it to make decisions about my next instructional steps. Better than reading quiz scores, this information is useful for all the right reasons. I've done this same thinking for each of my learning goals to make sure I collect data in my grade book that helps me and my students see their progress and growth (Figure 5.5). See Online Resources 2.1 and 2.2 for spreadsheets that line up this planning work with the planning in Chapters 2 and 3.

Figure 5.5 Grade book data for each learning goal

Learning Goal	I will know students can do this if they	I will find evidence of this learning in	So I will collect in the grade book
1. The student is a reader with a vibrant, self-directed reading practice that will continue beyond my classroom.	• Read more books than they initially thought possible. • Create lists of books to read in the future. • Read books that matter to them.	• Students' weekly reading check-in responses • Reading conference conversations • Observations of students' daily silent reading • Writer's notebook pages about reading progress	• Weekly reading check-in data • Conference notes
2. The student writes to think through life, to pull ideas together, to say something important to a targeted audience and for a specific purpose. The student is intentional about form and flexible to meet the changing needs of audience and purpose.	• Make independent decisions about the form their writing needs to take depending on their intended audience and purpose. • Write about topics that matter to them.	• All writing tasks and the writer's memos that accompany them • Writing conference conversations • Writer's notebook work	• Notes about what students choose to write • Conference notes
3. The student revises extensively to improve a piece of writing.	• Work on individual pieces of writing over lengths of time, achieving several different drafts.	• Thorough revisions, the major semester piece of writing, and the writer's memos that accompany them • Writing conference conversations	• Notes about what students work on in each round of revision • Conference notes

Learning Goal	I will know students can do this if they	I will find evidence of this learning in	So I will collect in the grade book
4. The student asks complex questions and persists to research answers to them.	• Stick with a singular research topic that interests them over a period of time, beginning with a research question of their own design.	• All writing tasks and the writer's memos that accompany them • Major semester piece of writing • Final semester presentation • Conference conversations • Writer's notebook work	• Notes about what students choose to write • Conference notes
5. The student seeks out mentor texts—for writing, for text form, for thinking, for reading—and uses those mentor texts to grow.	• Locate their own mentor texts to help them think through a writing or reading task that they are taking on.	• Writer's memos that accompany all writing tasks • Writer's notebook work • Conference conversations	• Notes about how students use mentor texts • Conference notes
6. The student maintains a writer's notebook as an important thinking and reflecting space.	• Bring writer's notebooks to class every day and work with them carefully. • Show evidence of thinking and reflection in their notebooks, inspired by what we do in class. • Turn to their notebooks to do this work without direction from me.	• Writer's notebook work • Seeing writer's notebooks in class every day • Students' reflections on how their notebooks are working • Conference conversations • Checking for work completed in notebooks	• Checks of writer's notebook tasks • Conference notes

(continues)

Figure 5.5 Grade book data for each learning goal *(continued)*

Learning Goal	I will know students can do this if they	I will find evidence of this learning in	So I will collect in the grade book
7. The student takes risks to learn.	• Take risks in class discussions. • Take risks in pieces of writing. • Take risks in the books they choose to take on. • Make mistakes and learn from them.	• Students' reflections (writer's memos, weekly reading check-in Google Form, six-week progress self- evaluations) • Conference conversations • My notes on whole-class discussions	• Notes about what students choose to write • Data from weekly reading check-ins • Six-week progress self-evaluation data • Conference notes • Notes on student participation in whole-class discussion
8. The student is a positive community member: provides high-quality feedback to peers on their writing, participates earnestly in small-group and whole-group conversations, moves through our classroom spaces (physical and digital) with kindness.	• Create a positive, vibrant classroom community. • Listen to each other. • Take great care in responding to each other's work. • Share their ideas with each other in class conversations. • Help each other through struggle and support each other's work. • Disagree kindly.	• Observations of students in class • My notes on whole-class discussions • Conference conversations • Stopping in for conversations with groups of students • Peer feedback found in margin notes on students' work	• Notes on student participation in whole-class discussion • Conference notes • Notes about quality of feedback to peers

Learning Goal	I will know students can do this if they	I will find evidence of this learning in	So I will collect in the grade book
9. The student demonstrates successful student habits: meeting deadlines, reading and following instructions, asking questions, seeking help and support, and managing digital tools and digital spaces effectively to keep track of work.	• Hit deadlines. • Turn in work that shows they have read and followed instructions. • Ask questions when they have them. • Seek out help and support when struggling. • Figure out and use our digital tools/spaces. • Persist in working through confusion regarding how a digital tool/space works. • Use digital tools and spaces consistently and effectively for class work and collaboration.	• Google Classroom records of who hit/didn't hit assignment deadlines • My notes on which students I had to return work to so they could review the instructions • Conference conversations • Students' reflections (writer's memos, weekly reading check-in Google Form, six-week progress self-evaluations) • Student use of Google Classroom • Access to the electronic grade book	• Data on completion of assignments (including timeliness and attention to instructions) • Conference notes • Data from weekly reading check-in • Notes on revision work
10. The student practices effective self-reflection, self-evaluation, and metacognition. Students know what they already know, what they want and need to know, what they've learned, and how well they've learned it.	• Use learning goals throughout the year to help them think about, plan, and evaluate their own learning.	• Plans that map out students' individual learning journeys • Writer's notebook pages tracking learning • Six-week progress self-evaluation • Conference conversations	• Six-week progress self-evaluation data • Conference notes

Navigating Obstacles 5.2

I'm not sure my grade book will do anything but record numbers and points.

You might be surprised if you play around to get a sense of what else is possible. I can type anything I want in the score box for an assignment in my grade book—a word, a phrase, a date. I'll get a warning that what I typed wasn't a valid entry, but it will remain, and anyone who looks at my grade book can see it.

If you find that you really can only type in numbers, then train your students to read them using a key that lines up the numbers with more meaningful qualitative descriptors. Or if there are required categories that organize your grade book data (formative assignments vs. summative assignments, for example), see if you can create any additional categories that don't calculate into the grade that you could use for words-based data.

If you aren't able to use hacks like these, you might be able to get some functionality opened up if you ask the right person in your school or district. Your grade book may be a powerful data collection and reporting tool with features you don't even know about yet. Every year I learn something new I can do with my grade book program that I did not think was possible before.

Take Control of the Math Machine

Unless your whole school is stepping away from grades, you'll still need to have some math reflected in your grade book. My school pulls athletic eligibility reports from grade books every week, and the administration runs frequent data reports to look for trends and areas where we need to offer students more support.

Because I can't refuse to put number data in my grade book, I quantify the only thing that's really quantifiable: whether or not students are keeping up with their work. The math machine still spits out an overall percentage for each student, but those numbers are not my students' grades. Instead, I recast the percentage as a metric that lets students know if they're keeping up with the work or not—a completed work percentage. And this is not grading based merely on completion; the percentage becomes only one data point of several a student and I will consider when determining a final semester grade.

I have to train my students—and other grade book users—to read that overall percentage differently. Rather than a constantly calculating, high-stakes grade, I tell them it's simply a status update, like a progress bar you might see as you wait for software to load on your computer. Their job is to keep the percentage at 100 percent. If it's not, something is missing or incomplete, and they need to figure out what it is and take care of it. This is enough number data for athletic eligibility purposes and for parents, counselors, or any other stakeholder to know if the student is keeping up with the work. If you're required to post a certain number of "grades" per week, this kind of completion data will most likely meet that requirement.

I use the importance of the grade book percentage in my school community to my advantage by thinking carefully about how the completed work percentage will function. For example, if I have a student who has chosen not to complete a major task, like a revised paper, then I want the completion percentage to take a bigger hit than if the student forgot to do a day-to-day task, like an entrance ticket for a Socratic Seminar. The revision task represents possibly weeks of writing back and forth between me and the student and is also one task that enables students to work on several learning goals for the course. If students are not doing the most important work of the class, the completion percentage needs to reflect it. To that end, I have different weighted categories, and if a student does not complete some of the major work for the class, the huge dive in the completion percentage creates an amount of alarm that gets that student to act quickly to get the work done (Figure 5.6).

Figure 5.6 Grade book categories

Category	Calculates into grade book percentage?	Weight of category
1. Semester grade negotiated by student and teacher at end of semester	Yes	99%
2. Completion of major assignments	Yes	0.75%
3. Completion of weekly drafts	Yes	0.2%
4. Completion of minor assignments	Yes	0.05%
5. Notes on revisions	No	n/a
6. Conference notes	No	n/a
7. Weekly reading check-ins	No	n/a

Nothing goes into this category until the end of the semester, at which point the semester grade, whatever it is, pretty much nullifies the other numbers. I enter the semester grade as one assignment in the semester grade category.

Categories 2–4 drive the grade book percentage during the semester. They capture how well students are keeping up with their work. Major assignments are weighted significantly more because they reflect the most important work I ask students to do.

I collect qualitative notes in the comment field for each assignment in categories 5–7, and they do not calculate into the grade book percentage. It's particularly important that category 7 does not calculate because I need my students to be honest with me about their weekly reading. If they're not, then I don't have an accurate picture of how well they are building their reading practice.

If there's an emphasis on numbers anywhere in the grade book, students will focus on them, so when you can, develop your own scale or set of marks that lets you enter words in the score box instead of numbers. Words like *complete, almost, keep at it, partial, review instructions, missing*, or *cannot* provide much more information to students about how they are doing.

It's a good idea to provide to students a clear key to read what you record in the grade book, especially if it's different from what they are used to (Figure 5.7). I've made my own set of "assignment marks" (as our data management system calls them) so that *complete* registers as 100 percent, *almost* as 90 percent, *keep at it* as 80 percent, *partial* as 75 percent, *review instructions* as 50 percent, and *missing* and *cannot* as zeroes. With these custom marks, my grade book uses words to show what percentage of the work a student has completed.

Figure 5.7 Key to what you'll see in the grade book

The number you see in the grade book as we move through the semester is *not* a student's grade. It is a number that reflects how much of the assigned class work the student has completed. If that number is not 100 percent, the student has something that needs to be attended to.

If you look up the full detail for a student, you will see many individual notes in the "comments" column that tell a more detailed story than numbers can of that student's progress. Here's an example:

Category: Completion of Weekly Drafts (weight: 0.2)					
Assignment	**Due date**	**Points possible**	**Score**	**%**	**Comments**
Weekly draft 1	1/13	20	Complete	100	You wrote a response to *A Place to Stand* (the film) about the moments in Jimmy's experience that you think most inspired his growth.
Weekly draft 2	1/20	20	Partial	75	You started writing an argument arguing against the school board's decision to extend the start time for high schools next year. Please re-submit once you write more beyond your introduction.
Weekly draft 3	1/27	20	Complete	100	Late Turned in 1/29; I cannot open the file attached—can you reattach your doc? Resubmitted 1/30. You wrote a personal narrative about your own struggles to focus in school.
Weekly draft 4	2/10	20	Rev. inst.	50	You wrote two poems this week. But there's no writer's memo. Please add and resubmit.

The take home message? → Open up the full detail on a student's grade data so you don't miss the specific qualitative data record that I'll build. I think you'll find it much more informative than a series of numbers. It will become the story of a student's journey as a reader and writer.

These are the words you'll see in the grade book under the "score" column for individual tasks instead of points/numbers:

- **T = Turned in.** I see that the student has submitted something to me but I've not yet had a chance to look at it.

- **Complete** = I got it, read it, responded to it (if relevant), and the student has no more work to do on the task

- **Almost** = The student is almost there on a revision. Maybe just a few more things to take care of before it's complete.

- **Keep at it** = I took a look at a student's resubmitted revision and there is still more work to do.

- **Partial** = I got it, read it/took a look at it, left the student some comments, and the student gets to keep working on the task.

- **Rev. inst. = Review instructions.** I got it but there is something critical missing. Maybe a writer's memo. Or maybe the student forgot to revise in suggesting mode. Review the instructions for the assignment and make sure everything is done as described.

- **Missing** = I haven't seen the task yet and the due date for it has passed. The student can still complete it. Let me know how I can help!

- **Cannot** = The student cannot complete the missing task—either because of a missed late work deadline for it (one week past the due date for weekly drafts or weekly timed essays) or it was something necessary for what we were doing in class on a particular day and it makes no sense for the student to do it after the fact.

You will also see some tags on assignments:

- **Late** = The student turned it in but past the due date. There's no grade penalty on the assignment (remember—no grades on individual assignments in this class) but late work could have an effect on the semester grade when the student and I negotiate to determine it. A key focus of this class is managing time to meet deadlines.

- **Had to review instructions** = I couldn't respond to the work when the student first turned it in because something was amiss (see "Rev. instr."). There's no grade penalty on the assignment (remember—no grades on individual assignments in this class) but this could affect the grade at semester. If students are not paying close attention to details on their work,

Figure 5.7 Key to what you'll see in the grade book *(continued)*

they are not doing their absolute best work. Slow down, focus on the details, make sure to follow instructions.

And there will also be some different things in the "score" column:

* **A date:** There's a note in the comment box that I entered on that particular date.

* **Yes/no:** Yes, the student met the weekly reading goal of two to three hours of reading per week outside of class, or no, the student did not meet that weekly reading goal. There's a note in the comment box with more information.

* **Reading + date or writing + date:** I had a reading or writing conference with a student and there is a note about our conversation in the comment box/column. These notes are often in the student's own words.

Progress reports:

Although the percentage you see in the grade book is not a student's grade, the grade you'll see on each six-week progress report may seem to mismatch that percentage. Students will determine their own progress report grades that take into account other factors alongside the completed work percentage.

My words-based set of assignment marks means that what goes into the grade book on an individual assignment is not static. I update the word to describe where students fall in the process as they keep working. They might start with *partial* but can definitely end up at *complete*. In this way, I honor the process of learning, recognizing that growth means working at something again and again. Students focus on the work rather than the grade. It frees them to take risks. It reduces their stress. They are not worried about losing points and can instead see their work for what it is so they can focus on making it as strong as possible.

Navigating Obstacles 5.3

What if I just don't have time to collect the word-based data in my grade book?

Think about this: choosing numbers to evaluate student work may take more time and energy than it does to provide descriptive statements about student work. If I'm describing instead of evaluating, I can actually work faster because I don't have to expend brain energy deciding where my students' work falls on a predetermined scale and then justifying the decisions I make.

And remember, students can help you collect the word-based data you need. It takes me fewer than 5 minutes per class to copy and paste my students' weekly reading check-ins into my grade book, and the data are in the students' own words.

Imagine What You Can Do with Your Grade Book

When I first started shifting away from points and percentages, it was difficult for me to visualize alternative ways to approach my grade book data. You might feel that way too, so I've included some examples here of qualitative grade book data to help you imagine possibilities that might work for you (Figures 5.8 through 5.15). In each example, we'll consider some of what the data shows us about the student.

Figure 5.8 Data tracking Kate's writing over several weeks

Category: Completion of Weekly Drafts (weight: 0.2)					
Assignment	**Due date**	**Points possible**	**Score**	**%**	**Comments**
Weekly draft 1 (feature topic piece)	8/29	20	Complete	100	You wrote to explore two possible topics: mountain/climbing disasters and baseball trading.
Weekly draft 2 (piece about *Into the Wild*)	9/7	20	Complete	100	Deadline extended to 9/8; you wrote a public service announcement warning people about the dangers of going into the wild.
Weekly draft 3 (narrative about you)	9/12	20	Complete	100	You worked on a college application essay that you had already written about your struggles during your middle school years.
Weekly draft 4 (second narrative about you)	9/21	20	Complete	100	You revised last week's piece. There's a new intro!
Weekly draft 5 (interview + anecdote)	10/3	20	Complete	100	Late. Turned in 10/4; you wrote about the experiences the person you interviewed has had climbing.
Weekly draft 6 (summary/ response of a research source)	10/17	20	Complete	100	You worked with a source about climbing that provides some key information you can't collect with interviews.
Weekly draft 7 (explain something complicated)	10/24	20	Complete	100	You wrote to explain how to set anchors when climbing.

Week after week, you can see the story of Kate's journey as a writer emerging (Figure 5.8). She started with a piece exploring two possible topics for her feature article, and you can see she landed on climbing because her later drafts work on different angles of it. You can see that she took the two-week personal narrative focus to clean up an actual college application essay she's been working on for a while.

The spreadsheet view enables me to see at a glance which students are keeping up and which are not so I know where I need to offer support (Figure 5.9). The box marked *Cannot* tells me that student 4 didn't complete weekly draft 2 and also missed the one week late due date to complete it. At that point, I want students to focus on keeping up with the current and future work rather than getting over-whelmed by past work to make up. That student hit the deadline for draft 3 but has missed the first deadline on draft 4. Seeing this, I can offer some support to help the student be sure to not miss the one week late due date again.

Figure 5.9 Spreadsheet view tracking students' writing over several weeks

Name	Weekly draft 1	Weekly draft 2	Weekly draft 3	Weekly draft 4
Student 1	Complete	Complete	Complete	Complete
Student 2	Complete	Complete	Complete	Complete
Student 3	Complete	Complete	Complete	Rev. instr.
Student 4	Complete	Cannot	Complete	Missing

Another helpful feature of my grade book on the spreadsheet view is that whenever I hover my cursor over one of these score boxes, if there's a comment associated with the assignment, it pops up. This enables me to look at the qualitative notes I have on individual students from this spreadsheet view. I could hover the cursor over the *Rev. instr.* and see my note about whatever it is the student forgot to include.

Figure 5.10 Data tracking one student's completion of minor tasks over several weeks

Completion of Minor Tasks (weight: 0.05)					
Assignment	**Due date**	**Points possible**	**Score**	**%**	**Comments**
Had writer's notebook	8/20	10	Complete	100	
Reading comprehension check, "The Really Big One"	8/20	10	Complete	100	Score 16/18; you said you read all of it.
Writer's notebook task, three features	8/29	10	Partial	75	You still need to finish the task on the third feature. Show this to me when it's complete.
Reading comprehension check, *Into the Wild*, ch. 1–6	9/7	10	Complete	100	Score 3/6
Socratic Seminar ticket: college app essays	9/10	10	Complete	100	
Socratic Seminar: college app essays	9/10	10	Complete	100	You chose to participate in today's seminar by listening to the conversation.
Reading comprehension check, *Into the Wild*, ch. 7–12	9/14	10	Complete	100	Score 5/6
Plan for learning and growth in writer's notebook	9/21	10	Complete	100	
Socratic Seminar ticket: *Into the Wild*	9/28	10	Complete	100	

(continues)

Completion of Minor Tasks (weight: 0.05)					
Socratic Seminar: *Into the Wild*	9/28	10	Complete	100	You participated in today's seminar by speaking in the conversation.
Reading comprehension check, *Into the Wild*, ch. 13–end	9/28	10	Complete	100	Score 4/7
Had choice book	10/1	10	Complete	100	
Set up document for collecting research	10/10	10	Complete	100	

To assess their work habits (one of my learning goals), I keep track of pretty much everything I ask my students to do, so the data record becomes extensive. The example in Figure 5.10 shows only half of the semester for one student. Notice the reading comprehension check scores—they're there, but in the comment box rather than in the score box where they would calculate into the grade book numbers. The scores provide useful data: I might want to follow up with a reading conference to explore the lower scores. There are not as many qualitative notes as in the record of weekly drafts—the point here is to provide a picture of whether or not the student is doing the day-to-day work, a key strategy for maximum learning and growth. I can also look at this same range of assignments in spreadsheet view where I can see at a glance who is keeping up with the work and who is not (Figure 5.11).

Figure 5.11 Spreadsheet view of data tracking students' completion of minor tasks over several weeks

Name	Had writer's notebook	Reading comprehension check, "The Really Big One"	Writer's notebook task, three features	Reading comprehension check, *Into the Wild*, ch. 1–6
Student 1	Complete	Complete	Partial	Complete
Student 2	Complete	Missing	Complete	Complete
Student 3	Complete	Complete	Partial	Complete
Student 4	Complete	Cannot	Complete	Complete

In my AP Lit class, rubric scores are part of the data, so I've repurposed the "score" column to hold the date when I review subsequent revisions of the same paper. My grade book flags this as an "invalid score entry," but it lets me put the date there anyway. The comments beside each date capture the student's process with one piece of writing over several weeks, and the rubric scores embedded in the comments are from the 6-point AP rubric. You can see in Figure 5.12 that the first time I reviewed Greta's revision, I estimated the rubric score at a 3 out of a possible 6. The next time, I thought it moved to a 4. And finally, when it seemed she had completed the revision work, I placed the rubric score at a 5. All of this is helpful information for a student preparing for the AP Lit exam.

Figure 5.12 Data tracking Greta's revision work in AP Lit

Category: Notes on Revision Work (weight: 0.0)					
Assignment	**Due date**	**Points possible**	**Score**	**%**	**Comments**
First revision	11/30	0	Oct 16		You revised your analysis of the poem "Greetings." Work on concision, connections, and more development. Rubric score 3. Partially complete. Next revision due by Wed 24 Oct.
Second revision	11/30	0	Oct 23		You added a bit more warranting—there's room for yet more. Conclusion still needs to focus on the speaker. Work on passive voice and "use of." Rubric score 4. Keep at it. Next revision due by Fri 2 Nov.
Third revision	11/30	0	Oct 30		You added a bit more elaboration and revised out "use" to be more concise and worked on a few instances of passive voice. Rubric score 5. Complete!

Notice that the rubric score is the least interesting bit of data in this record. The descriptive notes reveal so much more about Greta's process and help us both see the journey she has been on in revising this one piece of writing. For example, she did a great job managing the due dates I set for next revisions, even turning the paper back in ahead of schedule. Also, I can see that Greta's focus was on development and concision—more detailed ideas and sentences that are not as wordy.

This category of data does not calculate into the grade book percentage. You can see the category weight is 0, and the points for each "assignment" also equal 0. And a note on the due date: my grade book requires I put in a due date but it's a variable one for this assignment—each student will finish at different dates depending on how many rounds of revision they need to do. I set a due date several weeks in the future at a time I hope most students will have completed the revision process.

In the spreadsheet view of students' revision work (Figure 5.13), you see that the box for the timed write revision indicates the status of each student in the revision process. Student 1 has completed the process after turning in the paper three times. The *Almost* in the score box indicates that student 4 has also turned in the paper three times but still has some revision work to do. Students 2 and 3 are also in process as you can see by *Keep at it* and *Partial*. As they move through the revision process, I update the box so it's not a static data point.

And remember, when I hover my cursor over one of the boxes with the date, the revision note I wrote pops up. I can see very quickly here what each of my students is working on.

Figure 5.13 Spreadsheet view of data tracking students' revision work

Name	Timed write revision	First revision	Second revision	Third revision
Student 1	Complete	Oct 16	Oct 23	Oct 30
Student 2	Keep at it	Oct 22	Oct 28	
Student 3	Partial	Oct 24		
Student 4	Almost	Oct 12	Oct 21	Oct 29

I also keep data on student conferences in another category that doesn't factor into the overall percentage but is a critical record that informs so much of my instruction. In the record of conference conversations, the due date for each assignment (i.e., conference) is some point several weeks into the future because there really aren't due dates for conferences. They happen as needed, so I enter the day they actually do happen in the "score" column. The "comments" column stores data the students write themselves. As I described in Chapter 4, immediately after a conference conversation, I ask students to fill out a simple Google Form where they write what we talked about in the conference and what their next steps are with the work. I set that field on the Google Form with the same character limit I have for the comment field in my grade book (240 characters), so I can quickly copy and paste from one to the other without having to shorten what students have written. Having the notes in a student's own voice is meaningful. I can see what Kelly took away from our conferences, and she can consult the notes if she needs a reminder about what we talked about. (See Figure 5.14.)

Figure 5.14 Data tracking conference conversations with Kelly

Category: Conference Notes (weight: 0.0)					
Assignment	**Due date**	**Points possible**	**Score**	**%**	**Comments**
Note 1	12/4	0	Writing Oct 4		We talked about what I should write my anecdote on based on the interview I had with Mr. A regarding my feature piece. Next I will listen to the voice recording of the interview and take a piece from it and write my anecdote.
Note 2	12/4	0	Writing Oct 25		I was struggling to figure out what part of my feature topic was difficult to understand and how I could describe it in a simple way. Now I am planning on writing about the ripple effect of the ecosystem, starting with a metaphor.
Note 3	12/4	0	Writing Oct 30		Doc Z helped me figure out how I am going to organize my feature piece. Now I have a better understanding of how I am supposed to write it and I am far less confused.

The spreadsheet view of conferences really helps me to plan because a quick glance tells me whom I've seen recently and whom I haven't (Figure 5.15). Student 4 is my priority based on what I see here. A reading conference with student 1 is also on my to-do list. And being able to see the notes when I hover my cursor over each box makes this view of the data very useful.

Figure 5.15 Spreadsheet view of data tracking conference conversations with students

Name	Note 1	Note 2	Note 3	Note 4
Student 1	Writing Oct 4	Writing Oct 25	Writing Oct 30	
Student 2	Reading Oct 1	Writing Oct 23		
Student 3	Writing Oct 4	Writing Oct 11	Reading Oct 22	
Student 4				

No type of grade book data could provide a complete picture of a student as a learner. That's why when it's time to settle on their semester grades, students will also turn to their own reflective notes in their writer's notebooks, their writer's memos, and the actual work they have done to uncover the full story of their journeys (as I'll describe in the next two chapters). But repurposing the grade book as a qualitative data warehouse is a powerful way to get students focused on their learning and growth.

This chapter concludes the planning work that we need to do before we place our students at the center of assessment in our classrooms. In the next chapters we'll explore how students can set individual learning goals, track their own growth, and determine their own semester grades in conversation with you.

Interlude

Semester Grade Letter by Jake, Grade 9, English Language Arts

Dear Ms. Broaddus,

This semester has been really fun and a big part of that is how your open to everything or jokes my friends or I say and we don't feel like your a glooming shadow over us.

When it came to reading *Of Mice and Men* a big problem is I kept falling behind. Every weekend I would read nonstop to catch up to where we were at because I am a procrastinator but also a slow reader. That is all my fault which I acknowledge, but that was the hardest part of my semester. That includes the drafts. Drafts were easy to me but the writers memos were very hard. I am not good at judging myself good or bad, and the memos really tested my skills. By the last two drafts I really got a hang of the memos but that caused the work I did on my writing parts to not come out as well. It also showed me the bad habit I had where I would never do my homework, which I have now fixed, and that would show in my writing.

Throughout the year I think that your class was really engaging and you really connected it to how to learn, and putting us with our friends was a really cool thing to do. But I found that paying attention in your class was not hard especially during *Romeo and Juliet*. You would always answer my questions even though they were weird and were super easy to explain. When it came to *Romeo and Juliet* doing the death stuff I was always wondering what was going on and you would always answer my questions and explain the answers in detail so that I could understand it. But before *Romeo and Juliet* I don't think the things we did brought out the questions in me and a big part of that is they were already explained, and I don't like when things are already complete and that was a boring part for me in the school year.

Claire-Maria asked students to write about what they're most proud of and also what didn't go so well. She asked them to consider their reading, writing, participation, thinking, and student habits.

My colleague, Claire-Maria Broaddus, breaks down the semester grade letter task for her ninth graders so they can tackle one piece at a time. See her instructions in Online Resource 7.3. She even provides boxes for students to write in, a visual way for them to organize their thinking about what they learned. And you can get a sense of the specific goals Claire-Maria had for her students based on the questions she provides to prompt her students' writing. See Online Resource 7.4 for another example of instructions catered to ninth graders for this same task from my colleague, Jay Stott.

Jake shows a lot of insight here about himself as a learner. Not only does this help him to see himself more clearly, it gives Claire-Maria insight into how she can better support Jake's learning in the future.

Being a student was really easy in this class because it all made sense to me and was easy to track. The entire time we did *Romeo and Juliet* I wasn't board. For *Of Mice and Men* I was but the way you taught *Romeo and Juliet* made it really easy for me to learn. I think what also made it easy was that it was really fun to do and read about.

During my reading this year I was always falling behind and never understanding it. If you asked me today what it was about I wouldn't be able to explain it because I was so confused. I also think that the book was really boring which made me not want to read it but then I had to cram it into the weekend to do.

When writing I was never good at the writers memos but good at the drafts. With the 10 we did I was good at the drafts with 7 of them but then I spent more time on the writers memos and they became really good, but that caused my work to be worse. The work was always hard to do because the prompts made it weird to do in my opinion, I think I always participated.

I was proud of all the thinking I did in class and was engaged all semester. And being a student I don't think I was that bad at, I have been late once and always come with a smile. I think we always had nice talks and I was never rude to you, if I was I'm sorry. I always had my writer's notebook, and caught up when I missed class.

I honestly believe that a 94% really demonstrates what I did this year it wasn't the best of the best but it was better than ok. It was good but not perfect. A 94.11 is a good grade and I feel like a 95% would be cool because its a plain number. I don't need it and I don't care if I don't get it but I like things rounded to five and also a higher grade is always good. In the end my year went really well. And I hope our curriculum keeps me questioning like *Romeo and Juliet*.

Sincerely,
Jake

I'm not sure how Claire-Maria responded to the grade Jake selected here, but his explanation of these numbers is illuminating. It points to the primacy of the number in students' thinking about grades. After two full semesters in a class with no points and semester grades based on learning and growth rather than a collection of points, Jake still says that a higher number is a higher grade, which "is always good." Helping students make the shift in their thinking is a relentless pursuit. We have to engage the conversation frequently.

The percentage Jake refers to here is a completed work percentage, not a grade, as I explained in Chapter 5. My colleagues and I have discovered that the completed work percentage is often (but not always) a pretty good proxy for the semester grade students select. As you'll see in her grade letter instructions, Claire-Maria asked her ninth graders to start with that completed work percentage and decide whether or not it could work as their semester grade. This simplified the grade selection process for the needs of her students. I'll talk more about adapting the task for your students in Chapter 7.

Chapter Six

Invite Students to Set Goals and Reflect on Their Growth

BEFORE WE GET INTO THE NUTS AND BOLTS OF HOW YOU INVITE students to set individual learning goals, think for a moment about your own experiences with goal setting. Maybe you set a goal to get more exercise or to learn a new language. Once you began work on your goal, you tracked your progress and you could see your growth, but you weren't really aiming for some specific point of mastery because exercising and speaking a language are skills that continue to develop as long as you practice them. Meeting your goals successfully would simply mean you could see how different you were from when you started, and then you'd set new goals to keep moving yourself forward.

If you had a friend who decided to work on the same goals alongside you, you wouldn't necessarily go about your work toward them in the same way. Maybe you decide to take four short walks a day and she decides to take one long one. Perhaps you listen to a French tutorial CD as you drive to and from work, and she chooses to watch a Spanish television station each evening. You would both be growing, but you'd be taking different paths to the same outcome.

When we think about our students' learning goals as readers and writers, the same principles of goal setting make sense—we're interested in growth, and each student has to find their own way to grow. However, in our current standards-driven context, there's a lot of pressure for us to document students' mastery of required standards. It seems an unquestioned assumption. In books about grading (Stiggins 2017; Schimmer 2016; Marzano 2000; Dueck 2014; Guskey 2015), mastery-related language is common, with phrases like these appearing often:

* mastery of each priority achievement standard
* student proficiency

* academic achievement

* measure of academic ability

* level of performance.

The assumptions reflected in this language lead to standards-based rubrics, standards-aligned grade books, and anything we might employ to help us document mastery, proficiency, achievement, or student level of performance.

In the years that I've worked to find a different path to grades, I've found this presumptive focus on mastery to be at odds with what students need to be full agents of their learning. The very first semester I stepped away from traditional grading, I asked my students what they thought the semester grade should reflect, and growth—not mastery—was their unanimous answer. Over time I've come to realize that my students were right. If my goal is to focus classroom assessment on what will be most useful *to my students*, then together we need to develop a system that accomplishes two important goals. It must do the following:

1. Focus on growing readers and writers rather than mastering skills or content.

2. Recognize that each student is on an individual, unique learning journey.

A focus on growth instead of mastery just makes good sense. If students think they have mastered something, they think they've made it. Done. Task accomplished. Let's move on. But the reading and writing skills we teach don't have beginnings or endings. The work continues. The learning never ends. A focus on growth reflects this. A focus on mastery misrepresents it. (See Figure 6.1.)

Mastery is also difficult to capture. Because each reading or writing occasion is a different context with different needs based on audience and purpose, mastery is a shape-shifter. For example, consider this Common Core standard (grades 11 and 12) for informational writing: "Use precise language, domain-specific vocabulary, and techniques such as metaphor, simile, and analogy to manage the complexity of the topic" (National Governors Association Center for Best Practices and Council of Chief State School Officers 2010). For his magazine-style feature piece, one of my students worked for weeks to figure out how to explain hyperspace theory to people who don't know what it is. I can describe how he thought carefully about which physics-based terminology he could use and where he needed to find more reader-friendly words. I can tell you that he experimented with metaphor after metaphor to try to describe the dimensions of the universe beyond the three most people know about.

Her grades have improved slightly but not enough to feel proud of them. The only upside is her English class. Her teacher is some hippie type with new plans for grading. She grades by watching and learning from her students as much as the students are learning from her. She created this step by step plan to get kids to improve.

This was exactly what Miranda needed. Slowly, she started thinking about school as an opportunity to learn things about life. She made a chart about learning goals. She has never done such a silly thing before in her life. But surprisingly, it's working. She writes down things she has accomplished during the year, and it makes her proud. She's reading her class books. But not just reading, she's comprehending. She looks through the text using thoughtful analysis to better her understanding about the book's purpose. By the time timed essays come her way, she actually knows what she's writing, not something she comes up with to give the illusion she read the book. In class, she has a B, which is not where she wants to be, but she's learning.

Before, she would copy answers, Sparknote books, and never care about meaning or themes. Now, she's learned more about humanity and morals from her class books then from any movie she's watched. She honestly didn't know she was even learning until mid-semester. Her wacky teacher actually did what she said she would. Her plan for learning and growth is actually making her improve. It was shocking. At this school, she didn't think she could ever be good enough, but a different approach to teaching might have just done the trick to get her passionate about books again.

Figure 6.1 Writing about herself in third person, Miranda reflects on her goal to actually read the books assigned in the course.

Did he master this standard? Perhaps. But all I can do with any confidence is describe what he did and help him see the growth he achieved. Even if I did have a sense that my student had mastered this standard, I couldn't take that sense of what his mastery looked like and apply it to the work of one of his classmates. Now I've got a different human writing about a different topic with a different purpose for the work. The needs of the domain-specific vocabulary for explaining things with analogies or metaphors are totally different.

Over the past twenty years, much of the research in the field of assessment has moved away from a simple focus on mastery to a more complex focus on growth. A seminal report in 2001 from the National Research Council, "Knowing What Students Know: The Science and Design of Educational Assessment" (Pellegrino, Chudowsky, and Glaser 2001), argues that advances in the sciences of thinking and learning suggest that "assessment practices need to move beyond a focus on

Navigating Obstacles 6.1

What about other stakeholders who expect the grade to say something about mastery?

When parents, car insurance companies, prospective employers, or college admissions officers look at a student's transcript, what do they expect it means? Is it an indication that students have mastered the learning of the class, or that they've done all of the work, or that they can play the game of school and would thereby make great employees, or that students are ready to handle the work of college? Because we all get to grades a little bit differently, an A never means just one thing and is always open for interpretation.

The transcript grade *is* consequential for students—it matters for college admissions and scholarships and even future employment. Regardless of how we get to semester grades, we cannot control which stakeholders will look at our students' transcripts and what they will read in the grades they see there. So I'd rather focus on making the journey to a grade as meaningful as possible for my students instead of centering on the needs of possible future people who *might* look at their transcripts.

component skills and discrete bits of knowledge to encompass the more complex aspects of student achievement" (3). Researchers have taken up this charge with learning progressions that assess growth over time rather than a student's status (i.e., mastery, or proficiency) at any one moment in time.

Learning progressions, according to a strict definition, are designed empirically, either top down, based on judgments of experts, or bottom up, showing the path students generally travel as they progress along a pathway of learning (Shepard, Daro, and Stancavage 2013, 160). Either way, researchers have focused on developing descriptions of student learning as a continuum rather than a destination, placing students at their unique starting locations on the continuum and looking for growth as they move forward.

Although I love the focus on growth reflected in learning progressions, I believe they are too restrictive. Having one learning progression for a standard still implies mastery, and a single learning progression articulates only *one* path to get there, despite the fact that students travel on unique, individual journeys as learners. In this chapter, I'll show you how I have resolved this tension and encouraged my students to find their own learning paths as they focus on their growth as readers and writers. This chapter invites you to do the following:

* Get students focused on behaviors that support their learning.

* Help students set individual learning goals.

* Invite students to imagine what success looks like.

* Show students how to map out their own plan for their learning.

* Teach students how to track their own learning and growth.

Focus on Behaviors That Support Learning

The first step to get students ready to set goals and reflect on their growth is to get them focused on positive learning behaviors. We have to attack this head-on because many students may have spent years focusing primarily on behaviors that enable them to collect points, regardless of whether they learn anything or not. To bring this into focus at the very beginning of the year, I make a chart on the board with three columns: things students do that result in points but not learning, things students do that result in neither points nor learning, and things students do that result in learning. I also give students a few aspects of student life to consider: attendance, effort, preparation, engagement, attitude, and quality of work (inspired by a chart in Wirth and Perkins [2008, 24] about characteristics of outstanding and average college students). In small groups, students discuss examples of behaviors that fit under each column heading, and eventually we collect their ideas on the board (see Figure 6.2).

Things students do that result in points but not learning	Things students do that result in neither points nor learning	Things students do that result in learning
• Copy work from another student.	• Confuse the instructions.	• Talk to peers during turn-and-talks in class.
• Game rubrics to figure out what you can do to get the most points with the least work.	• Don't do the work.	• Get advice from the teacher.
	• Don't show up to class.	• Ask questions to make sure you understand.
• Use SparkNotes instead of reading.	• Allow yourself to be distracted by your phone.	• Be engaged in class.
• Watch the movie instead of reading.	• Throw the teacher off topic.	• Be honest, especially about whether or not you understand.
• Plagiarize.	• Talk a lot in class about things you're not supposed to be talking about.	• Do assignments based on personal growth, not for credit.
• Get too much help from friends.		• Actually read the books.
• Do work for another class instead (because you're focused on getting the points in *that* class).	• Space out, put your head on the desk.	• Do research behind topics we talk about in class.
	• Listen to music with one earbud in.	• Take time to write a better piece of writing.
• Memorize/cram studying at the last minute.	• Don't interact with your classmates.	• Try new things.
• Half-ass an assignment to get it done even if you don't understand it.	• Don't look at the instructions.	• Listen.
		• Pay attention.
• Pick a topic that's easy but that you don't care about.	• Don't use class time well.	• Do work because you want to, not because you have to.
• Let someone else do all the work.	• Have an "I'm going to do it at home" mind-set.	• Manage time well so you don't have to do everything at once.
		• Be sincere with the work.
		• Jump outside your comfort zone to work on things you're not strong in.
		• Double-check your work.
		• Pick the most interesting book instead of the shortest one.
		• Show up to class every day, and on time.

Figure 6.2 Typical student responses in class conversation about learning behaviors

After the whole-class discussion, I have each student personalize the thinking by making a "More and Less" chart in their writer's notebooks. I ask, "From this list of learning behaviors you just made together, what do each of you want to work on, so you will learn as much as you can in this class?" In the "More" column, they write specific behaviors that came up in the class conversation (or were inspired by it) that they want to do more of. In the "Less" column, they list specific behaviors that are getting in the way of their success.

Creating this chart with my students teaches me a lot about the learners in my room, and spending time on this conversation lets them know that changing their point-collecting behavior matters. And we're going to work on it together. I emphasize that learning behaviors are something students *choose* to do. They are not about innate ability or intelligence or talent. Success is within their control. And whether they've focused primarily on collecting points or have never really found success at collecting points, all students will have a concrete, personalized list of what they can focus on instead—a powerful invitation to engage in reading and writing differently than they have in the past.

The first several weeks of school, those learning behaviors are all that I ask students to focus on. "Do all the work the class will ask of you and see if you can truly change your learning behaviors. No grades. No points. Just do the work and try to learn," I say. I use the grade book to keep track of the work they are doing, and the only thing that can negatively impact their semester grade is to *not* do the work. Once a week, students look at their "More and Less" charts and reflect on how they're doing—3 minutes to write and 2 minutes to chat, split between small-group talk and a few quick share-outs to the entire class.

Set Individual Learning Goals

My goal in the first few weeks of school is to generate a lot of thinking and conversation about learning behaviors that will lead to success. This thinking is an important foundation for students to determine what they want their individual learning goals to be for the course (from which students and I will determine grades). And since students will personalize individual goals from the course goals I've established, these early weeks also give students time to get used to the work of the class and see what the goals are asking of them.

Around the fifth week of school, I ask each of my students to choose three of the content-related goals for the course as their individual goals. I've asked students to focus on more than three in the past, and it was too much for the in-depth self-evaluation I want them to do. If they have to prove they've grown in five, ten, twenty learning goals, it becomes an onerous task, one they might even take shortcuts to achieve. I'm not interested in shortcuts. I want to see depth, analysis, reflection. But there's not a magic number. Depending on your students and your teaching context, you might have students choose fewer or more goals, and you might decide to give them more support as they select them.

I print out the goals and ask students to tape them into their writer's notebooks (Figure 6.3). We take about 15–20 minutes in a single class period for students to highlight their chosen goals and write on the page why they chose them. They share with the people sitting around them, and then a few share out to the whole class about why they chose specific goals. *My* goal is to cultivate conversation about learning and goal setting in my classroom.

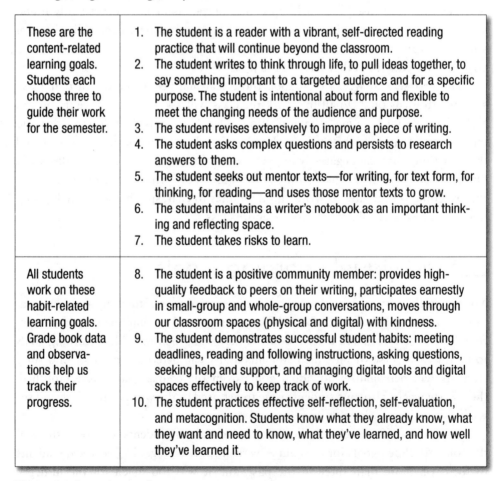

These are the content-related learning goals. Students each choose three to guide their work for the semester.	1. The student is a reader with a vibrant, self-directed reading practice that will continue beyond the classroom.
	2. The student writes to think through life, to pull ideas together, to say something important to a targeted audience and for a specific purpose. The student is intentional about form and flexible to meet the changing needs of the audience and purpose.
	3. The student revises extensively to improve a piece of writing.
	4. The student asks complex questions and persists to research answers to them.
	5. The student seeks out mentor texts—for writing, for text form, for thinking, for reading—and uses those mentor texts to grow.
	6. The student maintains a writer's notebook as an important thinking and reflecting space.
	7. The student takes risks to learn.
All students work on these habit-related learning goals. Grade book data and observations help us track their progress.	8. The student is a positive community member: provides high-quality feedback to peers on their writing, participates earnestly in small-group and whole-group conversations, moves through our classroom spaces (physical and digital) with kindness.
	9. The student demonstrates successful student habits: meeting deadlines, reading and following instructions, asking questions, seeking help and support, and managing digital tools and digital spaces effectively to keep track of work.
	10. The student practices effective self-reflection, self-evaluation, and metacognition. Students know what they already know, what they want and need to know, what they've learned, and how well they've learned it.

Figure 6.3 Learning goals

As we move through the semester, students work on all the learning goals I've established for the course, and my teaching supports that work, but the individual content goals they've chosen are the focus of their self-evaluation and reflection. They determine a baseline for each goal, track their progress, and document their growth. This is meaningful differentiation that offers accommodations for all students, including those who need more support and those who need more challenge. Selecting their own goals also aligns the students' course work with their aspirations for their future, an important benefit because as Stiggins (2017) notes, "To the extent that we welcome students into the decision-making process of selecting at least some of their own learning targets as they mature, we encourage them to pursue their own independent pathways to learning" (58).

Imagine What Success Looks Like

Once students have chosen three individual goals, they need a vision of what growth would look like (from their current baseline) so they can articulate the growth they are hoping to achieve. In a sense, I want each of them to develop their *own* learning progressions, individualizing the target end point for their unique learning journey.

To help students craft this vision, also in week 5, I form seven small groups and assign each group one of the content-related goals for the course. Their charge is to write a descriptive portrait of what success might look like for that goal. If it's the first goal about reading, for instance—"The student is a reader with a vibrant, self-directed reading practice that will continue beyond the classroom"—what would you expect from a student who had met that goal by semester's end? I ask students to use the work they've already done in class to help craft the portrait. For example, by week 5, my students have already filled out several weekly reading check-in Google Forms—what kind of evidence might someone expect to see on those forms for a student who has achieved success in this goal? I also provide the groups with some examples of former students' semester grade letters and grade book records that they can examine to craft their portraits.

After each group presents its portrait of success to the class, students use the presentations to write specific statements in their own words that capture what success will look like for each of the learning goals they have chosen. Here are a few examples of students' vision statements:

> ✳ "Reading is something that I really enjoy, it doesn't feel like a chore. My mind can be more focused on one thing at a time. READING IS FUN!" (for Goal 1 about building a reading practice)

* "I want to have several finished, important pieces I'm proud of." (for Goal 2, writing for meaningful purposes)

* "I'm proud of the contents of my writer's notebook. It is personal and reflects more than just my schoolwork." (for Goal 6, about maintaining a writer's notebook as an important thinking/reflecting space)

Map Out a Plan

Once students have written and shared the vision statements for their three goals, next they need to think about the steps they will take to make their visions a reality. So also in week 5, I show students how to think about the path their learning journeys might take. I've found that doing these three steps in the same week (but not on the same day) gives students time to think in between each step, which helps them make thoughtful decisions about their work. By the end of the week, each of my students has a fully articulated plan for how they will work toward their goals for the rest of the semester. (See Figure 6.4 for an example.)

Being explicit about what they will do to meet their goals is important work. As Guskey and Bailey explain, we need "benchmarks" to assess student growth, "graduated levels of performance or developmental sequences that eventually will lead to successful achievement of the goal or standard" (2001, 113). The students essentially craft benchmarks that they will use to monitor their progress. Some plan specific steps they'll take to get from their baseline to their goals, others identify learning behaviors they'll target to help them along the way, and others set minigoals that will help them move toward their larger goals. Most of my students, however, have never had to think about how to get from one point to another in their own learning, so I make sure I take the time to do this important work *with* them.

Modeling the process, I start by choosing a content-related objective that is relevant to my own authentic work as a reader and writer. This past school year, I was writing the manuscript for this book, so I chose making my writer's notebook an important thinking and reflecting space as my goal (see Figure 6.5). Under the document camera, I drew a blank chart in my writer's notebook to plan out the learning I wanted to do and asked students to do the same.

Next, I wrote the goal in my own words on the chart, "The writer uses a writer's notebook consistently to help with writing," explaining that my tweak on the goal reflected the problem I was trying to solve. Some teacher writers get up every morning to write in the hours before school. This is not something that works for me. I do better when I focus on school during the week and clear one weekend day to hole up

Figure 6.4 Quinn's plan for his learning and growth

Stating the goal in their own words helps students to own the goals in a powerful way.	*This is the baseline, the starting point from which growth will be assessed.*	*Students identify specifically what they will do to get to their goal: concrete steps to follow, learning behaviors to target, or minigoals to keep in mind.*	*The vision of success statements go here.*

Each learning goal in my own words	Where I am now	What I'll focus on to learn and grow	Where I want to end up
Read more outside of school (goal 1)	I don't read as much outside of school as I used to.	• Find motivation to read. • Create reading schedules. • Create reading goals for myself. • Find interesting way to keep track of reading.	I want to spend more of my free time reading, for pleasure and for school.
Shape my writing with mentor texts (goal 5)	When I write, I just write what I'm thinking.	• Read different texts to get larger perspective of different writing techniques/styles. • Choose a specific text and write something using its technique/style for experience.	I want to use mentor texts to create a unique structure and style for my writing.
Take academic risks (goal 7)	I'm not much of a risk-taker, and I feel like that holds me back.	• Take risks when they're available. • Step outside comfort zone when I can. • Do this until it becomes comfortable.	I want to be comfortable taking risks that could benefit me or be a learning experience.

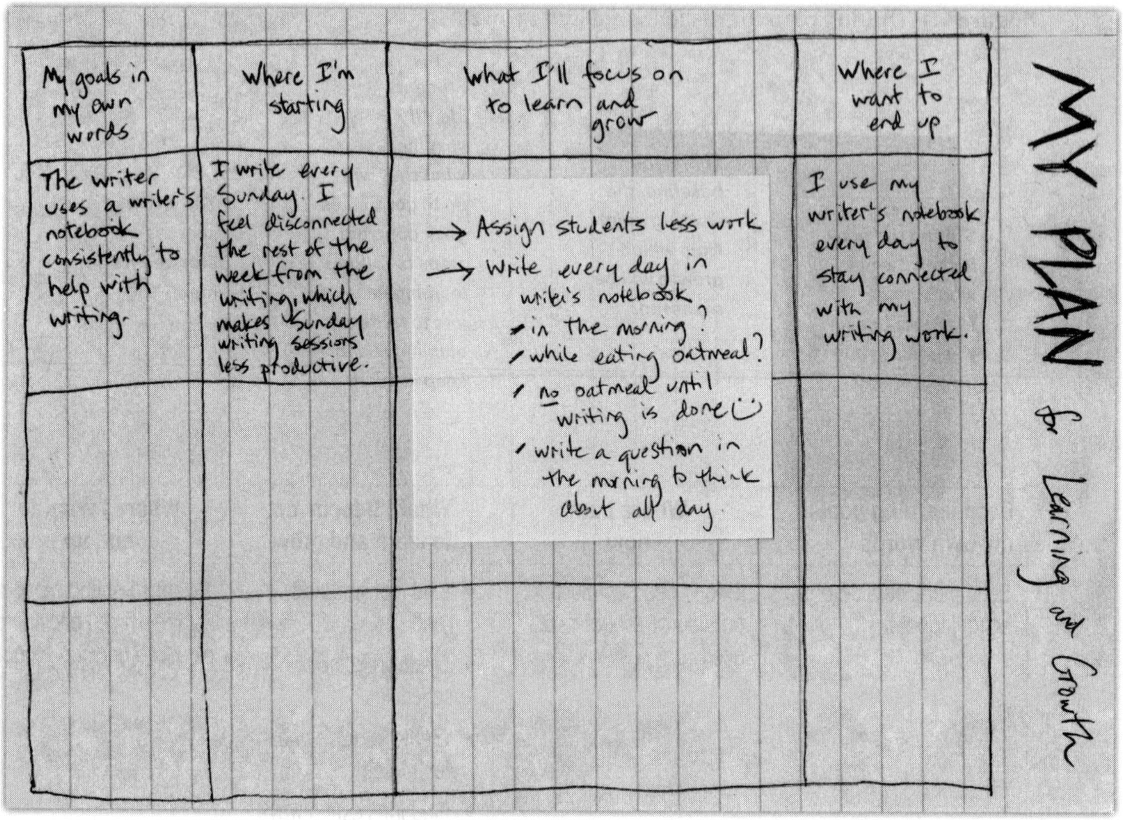

Figure 6.5 Planning my own steps to use my writer's notebook more consistently

with my writing for hours on end. This is a habit I've established successfully, but I often have a difficult time sinking into the writing immediately because of the time that has passed since the last writing session. Hence, I wrote that my starting point with this goal is: "I write every Sunday. I feel disconnected the rest of the week from the writing, which makes Sunday writing sessions less productive."

Next, I explained to my students that my goal was to use my writer's notebook every day to stay connected with my writing work (I wrote this on the chart), and then I turned to them for their help. "What can I do to get from where I'm starting to where I want to end up?" I asked. They talked in small groups first, and then they shared ideas as I recorded them on a sticky note in my writer's notebook, which I would use later to make my actual plan.

You'll not be surprised to know that the first suggestion my students had for me was to assign *them* less work so I would have less school work to do and more time to write. I thanked them for the suggestion, we laughed a bit, and then we moved on.

They said, "Write every day in your writer's notebook!" Well, yes, but that's not specific and concrete enough for me to be successful. I asked them when they thought I should write each day. "In the morning!" someone shouted. I reminded them about my morning oatmeal routine and asked them how I should fit in the writing alongside that. "Write while you're eating your oatmeal," one student said. "No oatmeal until you get some writing done," another student suggested. Mornings are hard enough as it is for me. Withholding nutrition until I get some writing done seems like a recipe for disaster. But the idea to write while I'm eating my oatmeal was something I thought I might try. I explained to my students that we had landed on a minigoal: a goal that is small enough to ensure consistent success. One of my students helped me to focus it even more. She suggested I write a question in my writer's notebook each morning that I can think about all day, thereby keeping my writing work rolling around in my mind during the week. This was exactly what I was hoping to achieve.

Modeling this thinking process is important for a number of reasons. The first suggestions my students gave me were not concrete enough to be actionable. As I pushed for more specificity, they were learning that *their* plans needed to be specific enough so they could actually follow them. Also, I'm showing my students that the learning goals for the course reflect the real work that readers and writers do in life. If their teacher is able to map out a path for the work *she* needs to do from the exact same learning goals they have, then the goals reach beyond what they are doing in the classroom.

Finally, doing this work with my students keeps me connected with what it feels like to do it. In all honesty, the "oatmeal thoughts" I decided to try didn't happen every morning. There were entire weeks where I did not write questions to myself alongside my morning sustenance. And those were the weeks where my weekend writing sessions got going a bit more slowly, and I knew I did not work as efficiently as I could. This frustration helped me to get refocused on my goals, look back at my plan, and remember what I had intended to do. My experience with the same work I'm asking my students to do shows me the ways the task might be difficult or challenging. I can see where students might need some grace along the way.

If you think your students might need a bit more support in this work, you could offer them statements that capture where they're starting (the baseline) based on your observations of their work. You might provide a bank of concrete steps students could take, learning behaviors they could focus on, or minigoals they could keep in mind to move from where they are to where they want to end up. Or you could select one common goal for the whole class to model the process and show them how to map out plans to learn and grow toward the goals they choose.

Navigating Obstacles 6.2

Shouldn't we be using the same benchmarks for every student so we can compare their growth and progress with other students?

You only need easily measurable, comparable assessment data if the goal is to rank and sort students via scales "on a continuum from good to bad or worthy to unworthy" (Wilson 2018, 15). When you shift the focus of assessment from mastery to growth, comparing becomes unnecessary and it gets in the way of students who are focusing—far more powerfully—on their progress in their own unique learning journeys. "Grading according to learning progress offers many advantages. First, it emphasizes individual accomplishment and improvement. . . . Second, it promotes individual responsibility. . . . Third, by viewing all progress as positive, it allows students to gain self-respect through their accomplishments" (Guskey and Bailey 2001, 114).

If students are constructing their own visions of success and monitoring their progress, they have ownership in the process, but the teacher *can* step in and nudge if students aren't pushing themselves to meet the expectations of a particular grade level or course. The process centers on growth, and it shows students that learning and growing are possible for each and every one of them.

Track the Learning

At this point in the process, students have individual learning goals. They know their baseline. They know where they're headed. They have an idea of what they can focus on to learn and grow. Now they need strategies to help them track their learning: as Stiggins says (2017), "When we help students learn how to engage over time in ongoing self-assessment during their learning, we help them form a link between their actions and their own academic well-being. In other words, we build their sense of self-efficacy in the classroom. And if that's not the emotional foundation of 'lifelong learner proficiency,' I don't know what is!" (90). Putting this into students' hands demands that they step up as full agents in their own learning.

Invite Frequent Self-Reflection

To build a reflective practice, use any opportunity you can to invite your students to reflect on their learning. Ask for writer's memos on every piece of writing they turn in: What were your intentions with this piece? What went well? What do you still need to work on? How did this piece of writing help you with your learning goals?

Reading and writing conferences are also excellent opportunities for students to self-reflect. Get them talking about their work—ask them to explain to you what they're working on and what help they need. Ask them to explain how the work relates to any of their target learning goals. Ask them to tell you after the conference what their next steps are with the work. Even turn-and-talk opportunities with classmates can be excellent opportunities for self-reflection: "Talk for a minute or so about how you're doing on one of your learning goals."

Writer's notebooks are great tools students can use to track their learning. If they set up a page for each learning goal, they can use that page to write once a week or so about how they're doing on that goal. Any time you ask students to turn and talk about their learning progress, you might ask them to record a few thoughts in their writer's notebook as well.

My students have needed models to imagine how they can use their writer's notebooks to track their learning and progress. Sure, I could provide premade templates and forms for this, but I really want my students to determine how to track their learning and to use tools they design themselves that work for them. I'm teaching more than just keeping track of their progress for my class—these are life skills. I show my students examples of how former students have used their writer's notebooks to track their progress, and then I challenge them to design some tracking tools that will work for them. They always come up with smart strategies I never could have imagined—bookshelves to track reading progress, two-column charts, open pages for notes, calendars, lists. The possibilities are endless!

Figures 6.6, 6.7, and 6.8, for example, show three very different tools students developed to track their progress for the exact same goal from my AP Lit class that reads, "The student actually reads a diverse range of literature because we are human beings and reading complex, imaginative works gives us practice in living a human life and imagining the experiences of others."

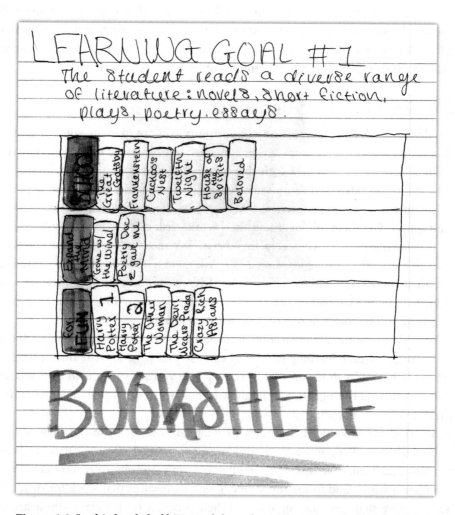

Figure 6.6 In this bookshelf, Hannah has planned out her reading for the semester. One shelf is for books she needs to read for school, one is for books she wants to read to expand her mind, and one is for books she wants to read for fun. As she reads, she colors in the books she completes, showing her progress in a single glance.

GOAL #1

Read and appreciate a variety of literature.
Read 2-3 hrs per week

Reading list:
- ☑ – Twelfth Night
- ☑ – House of Spirits
- ☑ – Beloved
- ☑ – Orange is the New Black
- ☑ – Turtles all the way Down
- ☐ – When You Reach Me

Book (s)	Week	M	T	W	Th	F	Sa	Su	Total!
Twelfth Night + OisNB	Jan 14th - 20th	30	-	15	30	-	15	30	2 hr
H of S + OisNB	Jan 21st - 27th	45	15	-	15	-	30	45	2.5 hr
H of S	Jan 28th - Feb 3rd	60	30	-	-	-	45	45	3 hr
H of S	Feb 4th - 10th	30	-	30	-	15	-	45	2 hr
H of S	Feb 11th - 17th	45	-	15	-	30	15	45	2.5 hr
H of S	Feb 18th - 24th	45	45	-	-	-	-	-	1.5 hr
Turtles all the …	Feb 25th - Mar 3rd	30	20	-	10	-	-	-	1 hr 'n
Turtles all the …	March 4th - 10th	30	-	30	10	-	30	30	2 hr
Turtles all the …	March 11th - 17th	30	15	15	15	-	30	15	2 hr
Beloved	March 18th - 24th	30	-	30	-	-	45	30	2.25 hr
Beloved	March 25th - 31st	-	30	30	15	15	60	-	2.5 hr
Beloved + When You…	April 1st - 7th	-	15	-	15	-	30	-	1 hr
When You …	April 8th - 14th	30	-	30	15	-	45	30	2.5 hr
When You	April 15th - 21st	30	45	-	30	-	30	-	2.25 hr

Figure 6.7 Julianna creates a record that allows her to easily see both the daily and weekly time she spends reading and monitor her progress to actually get through the books assigned for the class and the books she wants to read on her own.

Goal #1: The student actually reads a diverse range of literature because we are human beings and reading complex, imaginative works gives us practice in living a human life and imagining the experiences of others.

WHAT WORKS? EXAMPLES?	DATE
• Read 2-3 hours of Twelfth Night	January 23, 2019
• Completed Twelfth Night	February 13, 2019
• Read The Investment Guide for Teens	February 20, 2019
• Read House of Spirits	February 20, 2019
• HOS Reading comprehension check	February 27, 2019
• Read Beloved	March 15, 2019
• Beloved Reading comprehension check	March 15, 2019
• Read The Subtle Art of Not Giving a *****	April 24, 2019
• Read Now You See Her	April 24, 2019

WHAT DOESN'T WORK? WHY?	DATE
• Twelfth Night Reading check	February 3, 2019
→ Need to slow down and take the time to re-do it and check my understanding	
• Missed 2-3 hour reading goal	March 18, 2019
→ Distracted by other work	

OVERALL PROGRESS	DATE
• Read 6 books this semester	April 25, 2019
• Perfect score on Beloved Reading comprehension check	March 15, 2019

Figure 6.8 In dated entries, Alex records what works (to help her toward the goal) and what doesn't work, as well as notes on her overall progress.

Navigating Obstacles 6.3

What if students don't end up following the plan they map out for themselves?

It's impossible to predict one's learning journey, right? The plan is a starting point, but encourage students to follow the learning journey where it takes them. This is where it becomes vitally important to invite students to check in on their progress every week. In these check-ins, students can pay attention to the twists and turns their learning journeys take, make notes about them, and reestablish goals as needed.

Use Grade Book Data

Chapter 5 detailed how to make the grade book a qualitative data warehouse, pulling together descriptive data that reflect the work that students are doing. Students can use this rich set of information as another way to track their progress. When they look at their grade book data, I ask them to keep a few key questions in mind:

* When you look at the information in the grade book, does it suggest you've chosen goals that will truly support your growth?

* Where do you see evidence of growth?

* Which pieces of grade book data will you keep your eye on in the time ahead to track your learning and progress?

See Figure 6.9 for Quinn's weekly check-in data. I'm not sure how much Quinn used to read outside of school, but this record shows he's clearly not meeting the expectations for two to three hours a week of reading. By week 4 he is already behind on the assigned reading, and although he did manage to catch up and read two hours in week 5, his stamina was short-lived as he only read for an hour in week 6 (40 minutes of which was in class), the first week students were reading choice books. Quinn should keep his eye on the weekly reading check-in data in the weeks ahead to see if he can consistently hit the reading expectations and to look for any themes across the weeks when he's unable to meet them.

Figure 6.9 We looked at Quinn's plan to help him "read more outside of school" earlier in the chapter. Here's his weekly reading check-in data.

Category: Weekly Reading Check-Ins (weight: 0.0)					
Assignment	**Due date**	**Points possible**	**Score**	**%**	**Comments**
Weekly reading check-in, features	8/24	0	No		1 hour. I read three features "The Really Big One," one about immigration, "Syrian meets 'Syrian.'" I didn't read that much because I was focusing on other homework and wasn't looking ahead. I will read more features next week and will make time before I go to bed.
Weekly reading check-in, features week 2	8/31	0			Missing
Weekly reading check-in, *Into the Wild*, ch. 1–6	9/7	0	No		You said you read through ch. 2 and spent 30 minutes.
Weekly reading check-in, *Into the Wild*, ch. 7–12	9/14	0	No		You said you read through ch. 10 and spent 2 hours. Marching band and daily homework got in the way.
Weekly reading check-in, *Into the Wild*, ch. 13–end	9/21	0	Yes		You said you read all of these chapters and spent 2 hours.

(continues)

Figure 6.9 *(continued)*

Category: Weekly Reading Check-Ins (weight: 0.0)					
Weekly reading check-in, choice book	9/28	0	No		1 hour. Lost Ski Areas of Colorado. I'm really busy right now and I've been using most of my free time for homework and catching up. In the next week I'm going to try to make time for reading. I'll read my choice book mostly.

After focusing on growth and tracking their individual, unique learning journeys (Figure 6.10), at semester's end, we're finally ready to engage in the conversation with students about their semester grades. We don't need to leave it to the math machine in our grade books to tabulate the final grade. The next chapter will show you how to harness the power of narrative instead to help students see what they've learned and where they've grown.

Figure 6.10 Here is an overview of the steps described in this chapter to get students focused on growth rather than mastery.

Week 1	Focus students on behaviors that support learning. • 15–20 minutes on one day
Weeks 2–4	Check in on learning behaviors. • 5 minutes on one day per week (3 minutes writer's notebook writing; 2 minutes conversation, small group and whole class)
Week 5	Help students set individual learning goals. • 15–20 minutes on one day Invite students to imagine what success looks like. • 15–20 minutes on one day Show students how to map out a plan for their learning and growth. • 15–20 minutes on one day

Week 6	Show students how to track their learning and growth (include print out of grade book data to date). • 15–20 minutes on one day
Weeks 7–18	Check in on learning progress. • 5 minutes on one day per week (3 minutes writer's notebook writing; 2 minutes conversation)

Interlude

Semester Grade Letter by Ben, Grade 12,
Senior Literature, Composition, and Communication

Dear Doc Z,

"I hate writing," "I hate poetry," "I hate language arts." This is what I've told myself for the past ten years. For a decade I had convinced myself that I hated anything to do with language arts, besides reading (Unless I had to talk about what I read, then I hated that too). Whenever there would be a writing assignment, I would be sure to do the very least possible, only trying to get through the assignment as fast as possible so I could move on to things I wanted to do. Before I started this year I expected it to be a year filled with assignments that I didn't like, interspersed with exercises that seemed pointless, all while reading books that are overrated. I was surprised to find that this class was structured differently than what I had learned to expect. For the first time in a long time, I actually started to enjoy writing.

It took a long time to figure out what was different. At the beginning of second semester, I started to come to a conclusion. It was the rules. The being told what to write, being told how to write, all encapsulated in a time limit that only served to keep the class moving forward regardless of other circumstances. This class was one of the first opportunities that I had since first grade to do things that I wanted to do instead of stick to strict guidelines that my teachers had laid out for me. It's not like there weren't any rules, but they were generally laxer than they had been. Once I had figured this out that immediately gave me my first goal of the semester: Write more in my notebook.

Ben doesn't say this here, but I have to wonder if it was the points in past classes as well. Often the "being told what to write, being told how to write" comes along with a threat of lost points for noncompliance that forces students to do the work.

Ben set himself up with a very measurable minigoal, writing once per week outside of class in his writer's notebook. He is honest here that he didn't meet this consistently, but he is able to describe some ways the notebook writing helped him grow as a writer.

If the problem was being told what and when to write, then being able to write whatever, whenever should be an easy step in the right direction. Turns out writing once a week is really easy to forget about. On more than one occasion writing just completely slipped my mind, and I ended up writing nothing that week. The things I did write often weren't anything especially insightful or interesting, but they did help me keep my thoughts in order, which was much more helpful than I had imagined. When I did use my writing to try and work out something I was thinking on, I also found that it was extremely helpful. For example, in one of my entries, I was trying to find something to write about for *A Place to Stand* and was having trouble finding any topics, so I decided to write down anything I thought of, good or bad. I ended up writing almost a full page on a topic that I didn't think would go anywhere, which I eventually used for one of my papers. Seeing how much this has helped me organize my thoughts, I think it may even be something that I want to incorporate into my life after I leave highschool.

My second goal for the semester was actually a holdover from the previous semester. I didn't think I had done well enough to warrant marking "Find more questions and themes in what I read" complete. Part of why I chose this goal in the first place was because I wanted to get more out of books. I already enjoyed reading plenty, but it never really made me think. Last semester, if I was reading a book I enjoyed, I would usually get too absorbed in the story to stop and actually think about it, or if I was reading a book I didn't like, I would just read as much as I had to and immediately let myself think about other things. This semester I tried to spend more time after reading thinking about the things I read, rather than just getting through them and moving on. This approach ended up netting me three questions that I thought were interesting or thought-provoking, including the one I previously mentioned about *A Place to Stand* that created the basis of my essay. The line of thought I am probably the proudest of is one inspired by *The Road*. One of the main ideas of the book was the preservation innocence and purity, but if the actions you take to protect it lead to a world where there is no one left to be innocent or pure, then who are you preserving it for? Thinking about books like this has never been something I liked doing in the past, but after this semester I can't deny that I get a little excited when I think I've found a theme or some symbolism in a book.

I love that Ben chose to focus on one of the same goals he had first semester because he wanted to keep working on it. He was measuring his progress with questions that he could come up with after thinking about the reading.

My third and final goal for this semester was to take more risks in my writing. I wanted to push myself to try things I didn't know would work out, or try writing in structures that I'd never tried before. This didn't go well for every draft, and there were certainly a few that were just me falling back on old habit and using things that I knew worked, but there were also some drafts that I would say were improved from forcing myself to work like this. One particular example is my semester project, for which I used one of Lovecraft's stories, "The Call of Cthulhu," as a mentor text. One thing I noticed is that almost none of the relevant events were told through the main character's perspective, but rather through another source, like someone he was talking to, or notes that he had found, the main character only serving to connect the pieces of the story and provide their thoughts. I tried to use the same idea in my story, having the main character discover a journal and reading various entries. At the time of writing this, I'm not done with my final draft, so I don't really know whether or not it worked well, but then again, that's not really the point.

    Considering everything, I think that the work that I've done and the progress that I've made represents a B. I made good progress on all of my goals and I've done nearly all of the work assigned to me, I've grown my skills as a writer and as a reader, and while there were still setbacks and late work, I worked through or around nearly all of them. I wish I could say that this year went perfectly, but it didn't. There were times where life overwhelmed me and I had to get past it, but it's fine because I think that's just how we grow as people.

    Sincerely,
    Ben

Ben recognizes that the point is the process he engaged in. He challenged himself to try writing structures he had never tried before, putting himself in an uncomfortable place week after week with his writing. Given his realization that finally in this class he could write what he wanted, I love that he did not choose an easy path for himself.

Ben selected a B and I agreed with him. He recognized that there were places where he could have put in more work to result in more learning and growth.

Chapter Seven

Determine a Final Grade

AT SEMESTER'S END, THE PROCESS TO FIGURE OUT WHAT THE OFFICIAL final grade should be is a rich opportunity for students to reflect on their learning and growth. Here, for example, is an excerpt from Emily's end-of-semester grade letter, which tells the story of her journey toward one of her learning goals in my AP Lit class:

My greatest growth came in my learning objective to arrive at unique interpretations. My writing towards the beginning of the year was very focused on the 5 paragraph format, and was very straightforward and often dry for that reason. I was able to come up with interesting interpretations during class discussion, but not always on my own, and my individuality was not coming through in my writing. However, I had a breakthrough after we had the lesson about breaking the formula. At the time, we were working on *Pride and Prejudice*, in which I had many thoughts and personal connections to. So, when it was time for the timed writing, I decided to break the formula and talk about my personal connections, opening and closing with personal narrative. That essay worked, and was maybe my favorite of the year. After that, I was more comfortable and more able to really put my own thoughts into my writing. I wrote about Victor with a lot of voice and sass in the *Frankenstein* passage analysis. Then for my final essay, I examined systemic faults in *Frankenstein* with respect to Justine and justice, which I tied to the current sexual harassment allegations. I learned that instead of preventing personal bias from getting to the "right" answer, I should use personal bias to get to a more interesting and relevant answer. In this document, I stated that as one of my goals for this year. Allowing myself to be creative has transformed my timed writing process from a drag to an exciting challenge.

Emily's brief account captures the nuances of how learning to break formula in her writing enabled her to think more outside of the box—learning progress that would be impossible to see in a line of numbers in a grade book. Emily describes where she started, what happened next, and where she went from there. This string of causal relationships is narrative. It's a story. I had asked her for an argument about what grade she thought she should have, and she naturally turned to narrative to make that argument. Her letter made me think about the possibilities of story for my students to capture what they learn.

Wilson (2018) argues that "a claim that scores have grown is different than a claim that writing has grown, much less a claim that a writer has grown" (49). Emily's powerful story shows how she transitioned from an uncertain interpreter of literature who wrote formulaically to a reader who loved breaking formula to capture unique interpretations that she loved and owned. The story she tells about her growth *is* assessment. As Wilson says, "Conversations, observations, storytelling, and interpretations are assessment" (66).

The pages that follow will show you how to create space for this type of assessment. This chapter will invite you to do the following:

* Determine clear grade guidelines for final grades.

* Create a single document for students' learning journey reflections.

* Prepare students to write the story of their learning journey in semester grade letters.

Establish Clear Guidelines

If you decide to go point-less, you won't have a simple number scale to determine a final grade, but you will need some simple guidelines that clarify how you and your students will make grade decisions. There are two primary things you will need to decide:

1. what it takes to earn credit for the course

2. what it takes to earn an A.

I set a minimum collection of work that students *must* do to be eligible for credit for the course—four or five critical assignments that pull together the most important learning (see Figure 7.1). If students don't do even one of these, I tell them that there

EXAMPLE OF FINAL GRADE GUIDELINES

To get credit for the semester:

No major tasks can be marked as *missing* in the grade book:

- ▶ Intro letter to the teacher
- ▶ Thorough revision
- ▶ Major semester writing piece
- ▶ Semester final presentation
- ▶ Semester grade letter/story

Tell the story of your growth toward three reading/writing learning objectives:

- ▶ For an A: Your story of learning is detailed and compelling and describes significant growth toward your chosen learning objectives.
- ▶ For a B: Your story of learning shows growth, but the story could be more detailed and compelling.
- ▶ For a C: Your story of learning shows minimal growth.
  Base your story on qualitative data in the grade book, your reflective writing (writer's memos, writer's notebook, etc.), and various artifacts.

To get an A for the semester, also demonstrate A human being behaviors:

- ▶ Be a positive community member.
  This is based on teacher observations and student self-reflection.
- ▶ No late work. No missing assignments, major or minor. All revisions marked *complete*. Follow instructions. Completed work percentage in the grade book should be 100.
  This is based on data collected in the grade book.
- ▶ Stay on top of your journey as a learner.
  This is based on your own reflective writing.

And worry not: You cannot be knocked out of a particular grade category for one little thing.

Figure 7.1 Example of final grade guidelines

is no way I can see if they've learned enough to earn credit for the course. (Notice I don't say "pass" and "fail" because that's the language of the grading system.) In my past points-for-grades classroom, it was possible for students to pass by the numbers even if they did not do an important assignment. Now I'm able to take a very firm stand about the body of work students must produce. If a student neglects the work, there's no credit for the class, period.

For an A, students should first be able to tell a clear and compelling story about their growth as readers and writers that's supported by data, but I also want to make sure that an A means something more than that. I know that certain behaviors lead to learning—I call them "A human being behaviors"—and I believe A students should employ them. I tell my students that for an A, they also need to show that they have done all the work on time and followed instructions. They have to show they have contributed positively to the class learning community, have asked for help when needed, have used our digital resources to monitor their work for the course, and have reflected consistently on their own progress. I know that learning happens when students aspire to these behaviors, and that when they don't, their growth is not what it could be.

Of course, students listen to me explain this and hear, "If I have even one late assignment, I can't get an A?" That would be silly. And frustrating. And defeating. Life happens. Even the most conscientious student might need some wiggle room on occasion. But a chronic pattern of late work, or several missing assignments, or a consistent refusal to focus on the details of assignments brings down the quality of a student's work and decreases the potential for learning growth, thus keeping the student out of the A category at semester's end.

When you approach grade decisions in this way, you can consider each student's case individually and determine what grade makes sense rather than just letting the numbers in the grade book determine it. Guskey and Bailey (2001) explain, "While computerized grading programs mathematically tally numerical data, they do not relieve teachers of the professional responsibilities involved in making these crucial decisions. In the end, teachers must still decide what grade offers the most accurate and fairest description of each student's achievement and level of performance over a particular period of time" (133). This process centers our professional judgement as educators instead of giving it over to the math machines in our grade books.

To make this a more student-centered process, you may be wondering about negotiating the semester grade guidelines *with* your students rather than determining them ahead of time on your own. This seems like a good idea, but I have struggled to find a way to approach the conversation that doesn't take several class periods

Navigating Obstacles 7.1

My school uses standards-based grading. Will this work for that?

The answer depends on what "standards-based" grading means in your context. If it means that your grades line up with a set of learning goals, that's exactly what this process does. The difference is that this process centers on a simpler, more concise list of goals that you (and possibly your colleagues) write together rather than a long list of externally required standards. If "standards-based" means that instead of grading on a curve, your grades reflect each student's individual achievement of learning goals, then this approach can fit quite well. Students get the grade you and they agree to in negotiation, regardless of what grades other students end up with. If "standards-based" means that your grading practices are standardized among a group of teachers, then this is a journey you might all need to take together.

of thinking and work with my students. Of course, you may decide the class time is worth it, but here's what I've found: an intense, multiday conversation about grades makes it seem like I am emphasizing grades when my intention is to de-emphasize them. Students have called me out on this. They have felt betrayed.

Determining the grade guidelines is my job—I aim for something simple and easy to understand but that centers students as *the* users of classroom assessment data and positions them as the experts on their own learning. The grade guidelines are a scaffold that all students use to craft their own path to success, and every year my students help me to improve them—for example, they suggested the disclaimer at the end about not being locked out of a particular grade category for one little thing. This assures them that they can focus on their individual learning journeys, knowing that they won't get punished with the semester grade if things don't go perfectly for them. And once it comes down to negotiating with individual students for their semester grades, the guidelines are simply a starting point. Individual students have agency to diverge from them if they think their work and growth warrant it. They're usually right.

As you consider these two important questions—what minimum, essential work is required and what it takes to earn an A—imagine what you might craft that would invite your students to learn and make them experts on their learning growth and authors of their own stories about it.

Create a Single Document for Students' Reflections

I've learned that it is helpful for both you and your students to have one document that they visit a few times per semester to reflect a bit more formally on their learning progress. When it comes time for students to write the stories of their learning growth to determine their final grades, they need to have this all in one place. What you need is something that is easy for students to navigate throughout the semester and that has space for them to record all of the critical pieces such as the following:

* their chosen learning goals
* evidence of growth connected to the learning and growth plans they mapped out for themselves
* reflection along the way about where they are in their individual journeys.

My students actually have two opportunities to think about how a grade reflects their learning *before* we get to the final grade, and I designed a Google Doc to capture reflections at these two critical junctures (see Online Resource 7.1 for this document). At all three checkpoints—week 6, week 12, semester's end—I ask students to review grade book data, reflect on learning goals, and say something about the grade I should put in for them at that point. The first two grades—at six weeks and twelve weeks—are progress reports that I'm required to submit but are not recorded on students' official transcripts. Because of this, I can convince students to be completely honest even if things are not going so well at each of those check-in opportunities. For example, in his first progress report, Ben explains that so far, he's mostly been preparing to meet his goal of reading more, but not actually reading (Figure 7.2).

Grade opportunity		**Goal 1:** Read more
Progress report 1 **Grade selected:** **B**	**Where you're at in your plan for learning and growth**	I am in the beginning stages of starting my venture into my hopefully long reading career.
	How you know you're there (evidence)	I have opened an account of Overdrive, the school's audio-book system and am looking for a book to listen to. I am searching for a new genre to branch out into, I am thinking of business books.
	Reflect on progress and indicate plans for time ahead	As of now I don't have any progress on my goal however I am in the process of setting up my library so I have a set reading list. I will work on getting through all of them by the end of the semester.

Figure 7.2 Ben's first reflection on his learning goal to read more

The goal is for students to record information and reflections along the way that help them to be detailed and specific about their learning journeys. My student Phoebe, for example, was working on a goal to improve her writing on timed essays—a staple of AP Lit. She knew she got stressed and had a hard time thinking clearly in these situations, which made her writing feel forced and formulaic. Her plan for her learning and growth included the following:

* Come prepared for what I'm about to write.

* Practice thinking clearly and not getting overwhelmed.

* Develop techniques to use when organizing my writing in an unformulaic way.

Each time she reflected on her growth, she incorporated her plan into that reflection (see Figure 7.3).

Figure 7.3 With her learning goal related to timed writing, you can see how Phoebe's reflection at each grade opportunity follows her plan.

Grade opportunity		**Goal:** Write timed essays to practice clear and focused thinking
Progress report 1, first six weeks **Grade selected: A**	**Where you're at in your plan for learning and growth**	Practice thinking clearly and not getting overwhelmed.
	How you know you're there (evidence)	• I thought that the last timed essay I wrote was a lot better than the first one, and I managed to write it in a somewhat unformulaic way. • I came prepared for the timed essay on *The Great Gatsby* by looking through the text the night before and finding quotes that I could use in an essay about different themes. • I took a few deep breaths before starting my essay, and that helped me calm down and get focused.
	Reflect on progress and indicate plans for time ahead	Since I am getting better at writing in an unformulaic way during timed essays, I am improving at them and getting closer to my goal. I am pleased with how my last timed essay turned out, because although it wasn't perfect, it shows that I have formed a better strategy for writing timed essays.
Progress report 2, second six weeks **Grade selected: B+**	**Where you're at in your plan for learning and growth**	Practice thinking clearly and not getting overwhelmed.
	How you know you're there (evidence)	• I prepare for each timed writing the night before by jotting down things I want to remember and coming up with theme statements. • Some of my timed writings went really well and I was very proud of my work, and others did not go so smoothly. • The more I do timed essays, the easier it is to stay focused during the writing. I don't lose my train of thought as often as I did at the beginning of the year.

	Reflect on progress and indicate plans for time ahead	Although not all of my timed essays were great, I do think that I've made progress with this goal. I do good prep work beforehand, and I use the first 10 minutes to plan out my essays and get the ideas flowing before I start writing. I usually feel pretty focused while writing, but when I re-read my work my writing is often confusing and unfocused. In the future I'm going to work on keeping my writing more focused.
End of semester **Grade selected:** **A**	**Where you're at in your plan for learning and growth**	I'm about where I wanted to end up when I made this goal, though there is still improvement that can be made: developing techniques to use when organizing my writing in an unformulaic way.
	How you know you're there (evidence)	• Every night before a timed write, I write down important things, theme statements, evidence, or anything else that would be helpful for the writing. • My writings have gotten longer. I'm now able to write 2 or more pages single spaced, whereas at the beginning of the year I only wrote 1–2. • I've been happy with some of my timed writes! I was really proud of my *Cuckoo's Nest* essay and my essay on "Plants." • Doc Z gave me higher scores on my last essay than on my first. (3 on first and 5 on last) Though I wasn't super pleased with my last essay on *Frankenstein*, it went better than my first one, so there was improvement!
	Reflect on progress and indicate plans for time ahead	Timed writes don't seem like such a big deal anymore. At the beginning of the year, this was the thing that I dreaded most about APLit, but now I don't mind it very much. When I was able to get in the zone and focus on my writing, I had fun with it (kinda). I felt proud of my essay on *Cuckoo's Nest* and had fun coming up with my ideas while writing. However, sometimes I struggled with getting started on my essays. Next semester I think I will focus on developing strategies to plan out and start my essays faster.

My students are more successful in these self-reflections and can do the challenging thinking I'm asking of them as long as they understand the task clearly. Think about the kind of concrete support your students might need to do this reflective thinking about their work. Here are some possibilities:

* Show students exactly what the self-reflection you want them to do looks like. Model it with your own learning goals or with one goal the whole class is working on together.

* Provide sentence stems to help students to get started. Tell them to fill in the blank with something specific about their work so far:

» This _____ shows / means / suggests . . .

» Since _____, that means . . .

» I am pleased with _____; it shows I have . . .

» I am not so happy with _____; it shows I have . . .

» I am surprised about _____; it shows I have . . .

* Provide an example of a past student's (anonymous) grade book data and discuss which information relates to which learning goals. Choose one goal to examine more closely. Ask, "What does the information reveal about the student's learning and growth toward that goal?" Then help students to do the same thinking with their own grade book data.

Prepare Students to Write the Stories of Their Learning Journeys

Why stories? Maja Wilson (2018) explains, "We are the sense we make of what happens to us, and this sense making happens, in large part, through storytelling" (40). When students construct stories about their journeys as learners, they focus on their experience rather than on some supposedly objective measurement. Story is also natural to us. It is how we make sense of our world. In *Minds Made for Stories* (2014), Tom Newkirk says we can use narratives to make sense of what is difficult to understand: "When we employ narratives—and approach experience as *caused* and comprehensible—we gain a measure of control. We take a stand against randomness and fatalism and in favor of a world that makes sense" (34). How any human grows as a reader and a writer *is* difficult to make sense of, but we can attempt to do so by asking students to describe what they've learned in the form of a story.

I ask each of my students to write me a letter (in the form of a story) about their learning journey. (See Figure 7.4.) Why letters? Because a letter is a conversation—one person reaching out to say something important to another. A letter is also personal. Students write their stories for an audience—their teacher—who has been there with them every step of the way. The letters are a major assignment (required for course credit), and they essentially become portfolios as students pull together all the learning reflections in their writer's notebooks, the qualitative data I collect in the grade book, and the three grade reflections they have done at different points in the semester. In the Online Resources (7.2, 7.3, and 7.4) you can see how my colleagues have adapted this task for students in sixth and ninth grades.

Figure 7.4 Semester grade letter instructions

We use story to make sense of our experiences as humans, so I want you to explain which grade best reflects your work by *writing a story* that shows how you grew as a learner this semester as you worked toward each of your personal learning goals and the class goals. Since it's a story, consider the following:

* Are you the protagonist or antagonist of the story?

  » If you're the protagonist, who/what was the antagonist? (Possible antagonists include procrastination, other people, yourself, being too busy, the books, your smartphone, your teacher, the weather . . .)

  » If you were the antagonist in your own journey, what/who was the protagonist?

* Who are the other characters and what role did they play? (These could be authors you read, pod mates, teacher, people you talked to outside of class, etc.)

* What were the conflicts/obstacles you came across and how did you navigate them?

* What were the major plot events/moments of your learning journey? (Think about your progress on your plan for learning and growth for each of your learning goals.)

* What was the setting(s) of your learning story? (Could be a physical place or something like your writer's notebook or maybe in conversation or in your head while you were reading.)

* How about some dialogue? (Did anyone say anything to you—or did you say anything—that should show up as dialogue in your story?)

* What is the resolution of your learning story? How does it end? (For now—it continues next semester.)

Provide links and specific examples (even quotes from your work) as the details that will bring your story alive. Find the details you need for your story:

* on your learning/progress document

* in the grade book

* in your writer's notebook

* in feedback tables/notes/memos on your pieces of writing.

Note: There are sample grade letter stories you can use as models attached to this assignment in Google Classroom. You don't need to write a Pulitzer Prize–winning story. As long as it's true to *your* experience this semester, that's enough.

To give you a sense of how students move from the reflections they do across the semester to the final grade letter, here's an excerpt from Phoebe's letter where she writes about her journey to write timed essays more effectively.

If at the beginning of the year you were to tell me that I would enjoy writing timed essays by the end of the semester, I would have laughed in your face. Timed essays have always been something I've struggled with. They consist of two things that I have always been horrible at: staying focused and doing things in a timely manner.

At the beginning of the semester, I was really worried about the amount of timed writing that we were going to be doing in this class. But because there were no grades, I became less anxious about my writing, which allowed me to maintain my focus. The only people who were going to be reading my work were my pod mates, and I developed trust that they would be kind to my writing. Lisa and I often traded essays, and each time we traded I became less anxious about what she was going to think of my writing. She gave me a lot of helpful feedback, and talking to her about my writing became easier and easier.

The essays that I had the most fun writing were actually the ones that I thought were the most difficult. I thought that the hardest prompt we had was the prose analysis on *One Flew Over the Cuckoo's Nest,* but I had the most fun writing it. It took me a while to start my writing, but once I began, the ideas started to flow onto my paper almost at the same time that I was coming up with them. I remember thinking *Dang, Phoebe, that's a really good point.* This felt good! I couldn't believe it! I was having fun during a timed writing! From then on I approached timed essays more confidently, knowing that I had the ability to write something I was happy with in 45 minutes. Not all of my essays were great, but I suppose there's variation with everything.

I spent time prepping before each essay by writing down important things about the work, theme statements, and anything else that would help me in my writer's notebook. This prep work definitely played a role in my success. I was able to dive into writing quicker when I had theme statements ready to go, and I didn't need to waste valuable writing time sitting there thinking.

Navigating Obstacles 7.2

What if students ask to have a conversation with me instead of writing a letter?

Ask them to write the letter first, always. The writing is an important process of reflection and encourages students to do some powerful synthesis about their learning. The conversation should not happen until they have done this critical work. Another reason to ask for the letter first is this: if a student's letter identifies a grade that you don't agree with, you need time to reexamine the data and carefully consider the student's description of the learning journey before you respond.

Notice all the narrative elements in Phoebe's letter. There's a sense of one event leading to another, leading to another. There is a main character—Phoebe. There's a plot—she wants to improve her timed writing experience. There are other characters—Lisa and her unnamed pod mates who help her with feedback that increases her confidence. There's a resolution—she ends up actually enjoying the writing rather than dreading it. When we invite students to organize their learning with a narrative frame, something that is innate to all humans, they become the authors of their own learning stories, both in the classroom and hopefully in their lives beyond school.

The Elements of Story

The first semester I asked students for stories rather than arguments for the semester grade letter, I did the task myself first to experience it as an insider. I started with some targeted prewriting on a planning table where I listed the elements of story in the rows and then made a column for each of my learning goals. I shared all of my prewriting and my letter with my students, and then several of them used the same table to pull together their thinking.

Olivia's extensive table (Figure 7.5) helped her to write a very detailed, specific letter about her learning journey. For example, notice how she wrote the story of the role her cat played in her journey to her reading goal.

Another conflict in my daily routine was the actual way I would lie in my bed. My devilish but sweet cat, Kitty Kitty, is a lap baby. Every time I would brush my teeth, I'd come back to her waiting expectantly on my bed. She has no problem with sitting on my arms, and when I'd try to move them out from under her she would bite and paw at the moving lumps. This is usually very cute, but Kitty has been getting rather long in the tooth lately, both literally and figuratively, so those playful bites can also pierce through thick blankets. I'd usually admit defeat, succumbing to sleep with the light still on and the itch on my forehead unscratched. When I decided to change this aspect to make way for reading time, I also proved that although old dogs can't learn new tricks, old cats can. I took a trip down to the basement and brought up an extra pillow which I used to construct a throne fit for Her Majesty, and she took right to it. I could now read as much as I want, be it *Lord of the Rings*, *The Serengeti Rules*, *Born on a Blue Day*, or other texts related to my feature before bed.

Figure 7.5 Olivia's prewriting through the elements of story

My three goals →	Reading practice	Complex questions, research, persistence	Seeking and using mentor texts to grow
Protagonist/ antagonist	Pro: My inner reader Ant: Other school work, procrastination	Pro: My interest in the topic Ant: Wanting to stick with what I know how to do; research by reading scientific papers, write very information heavy	Pro: My drive to create a meaningful product I was proud of Ant: Sticking to mentor texts that I used for information, only branching out towards the end
Other characters	*Lord of the Rings* characters My Dungeons and Dragons group The librarians Sister practicing trumpet at 10pm	Doc Z, comments on drafts? My friend in band, my cousin; was interested in the topic because of them and wanted to do a good job	Doc Z, comments on drafts?
Conflicts/obstacles	Falling asleep holding the book, accidentally drooling on the corner of Two Towers Procrastinating assignments by watching *Law and Order* right after school Cat sleeping on my arms as soon as I lie down	Directing my general interest to an attainable goal that I could meet by research and writing Was scared to interview someone that I didn't know, chose my aunt to overcome	Reading broadly, not mining for information; took a lot of time
Major plot events	Sitting down with myself and deciding on the outline of my reading schedule Cleaning my bedside table Training kitty to sleep on her pillow	Interview? Finishing Feature, feeling proud of accomplishment that took me out of my comfort zone	Realization that mentor texts were actually helpful with structure, style, tone, voice, and not just for information/facts

(continues)

Figure 7.5 Olivia's prewriting through the elements of story *(continued)*

My three goals →	Reading practice	Complex questions, research, persistence	Seeking and using mentor texts to grow
Settings	In my room My hammock? School?	My room? Dining room table?	Dining room table? ah?
Resolution	I feel like a calmer human Reading has allowed me to escape stress rather than adding it to my life, one of the few activities that does that other than kittens Very motivated to continue growing in this area, I have a list of my next reads	Finished feature Proud I transformed my complex question into an attainable goal in my feature writing, took the necessary research steps to reach it, and I produced a final draft that conveys my message to the reader and has all the aspects of a great feature. I completed my feature, and during that process I learned many things about what it takes to write journalistically and not come across sounding like a scientific paper.	I chose "The Really Big One" as my main feature mentor text because of how I wanted to emulate the author's structure and command of data, stories, and personal voice. I used it by structuring the different parts of my feature similarly, and then I kept the author's style and tone in mind while writing. I plan to continue using mentor texts in new ways next semester.

I love Olivia's problem-solving here. Her dear pet was getting in the way of her achieving her reading goal. She listed Kitty Kitty's behavior in her planning table as a conflict, and "training Kitty to sleep on her pillow" as a significant plot point. From that planning we get this delightful story about navigating a unique obstacle to building a reading practice.

Not all my students plan as extensively as Olivia did before writing their letters, but as you can see in the excerpts from students' letters in Figures 7.6 through 7.9, the invitation to use story to make sense of their learning often leads them to unexpected places in their writing.

Figure 7.6 Occasionally, I show up as a character in students' stories, as seen in Kendra's letter.

All of a sudden a whoosh comes by; it's you crouched down to the level of my chair. My heart pounded profusely. I knew it was about the reading. You whispered, "How's the reading been going?" I could feel my face turn red with embarrassment. I stutter a little, "It's been alright." I lied. I made an ignorant excuse as to why I couldn't read a totally reasonable amount each week. Narrowing your eyes, you said, "Everyone has the same amount of time, it just depends on how you spend it." That shut me up real quick. As you walked away I thought: a teacher just called me out on my nonsense. This was the turning point in my reading habits. I knew I had to step up my game and take responsibility.

Figure 7.7 Mateo shows that students often discover how valuable their classmates are to their learning.

I began to ignore Annie's gossiping and Mike's randomness and talk to Elizabeth about what we were supposed to be talking about. I was very intrigued with what she had to say, and the great feedback that she would give back to me when I would speak about something. When we were analyzing *The Great Gatsby*, a book that I read too quickly over the summer, I heard a lot of great new things like symbols and themes that I had neglected like Gatsby's car, which symbolized extravagant wealth and a great argument for how Gatsby's love for Daisy wasn't true love. Rather lust and compensation for failure in the past.

Figure 7.8 The smartphone as a distraction, a conflict, an actual character is a frequent feature of students' stories of their learning. And students sometimes write about themselves in the third person to see themselves differently in their own stories, as Jakob does here.

Jakob had just started the first page of *The Great Gatsby* when he felt a sharp tug on his feet; he looked down and to his great dismay a phone dwarf was pulling on his leg. Jakob slowly began to slip into the phone dwarf's grasp, and Jakob was soon floating through the amazing land of Instagram and Snapchat. Jakob was completely entranced by phone Dwarf and under its magical spell. When he finally fought his way out of the phone dwarf's spell, he realized he had wasted hours of time. Slowly Young Jakob learned how to tame the phone dwarf and keep its temptation at bay. This was the first step to for Jakob to be able to interact with literature for long periods of time.

Figure 7.9 As Natalia shows here, students learn to zoom in on very specific moments that made a difference in their learning.

When we had a book talk in the library and the librarian brought up animal abuse a little light went off. I had found something I had a passion for. I started reading some books and found the book *Beneath the Surface.* This book inspired me a lot throughout my feature, and I learned that finding a mentor text doesn't need to be hard. I remember reading my book and this one chapter called "The Dark Side" really stood out to me. I realized the chapter was written through the lens of an orca and so I decided this would be a great way to use a mentor text. I decided to make my whole feature through the lens of different animals and thought it would be a great way to work on my goal.

Agreeing on the Final Grade

Coming into finals week every semester, I bristle at what I overhear my students saying about their final exams for some of their other classes. "I only need to get a 20 percent on the final to keep my A!" They think they don't need to prepare for that final, which means they are essentially blowing off a culminating learning opportunity. The end of the semester is not when students should be looking for ways to cut corners to preserve the grades they want. It should be a most meaningful time of the school year where students solidify what they have learned and articulate it powerfully.

The process I've described in this chapter *is* meaningful, and it may surprise you, but in most cases, I agree with the grades my students select. They do a better job at this than I ever could have anticipated. But when we don't immediately agree, I might do one of a few things:

✴ Reconsider my take on the student's grade. I take some time to review the data and consider if the grade the student selected is actually a better reflection of their learning and growth. Oftentimes, it is.

Navigating Obstacles 7.3

What if my students all say they should have an A?!

I have plenty of students who say that an A best captures their work for the semester, but my experience has been that I actually have fewer final A grades and more Bs and Cs than I had when I used a traditional grading system. I attribute this to the shift from a focus on collecting points to get the grade to having to do all the work, thoughtfully and completely, to get the grade. Every year I have students tell me that when they first hear about my approach to grading, they assume it will be a walk in the park, but that they quickly realize they were wrong about that.

* Point back to the grade guidelines and use them to clearly explain why I had in mind a different grade. Then I invite the student to convince me I'm wrong.

* Invite the student to do more work—if there's something critical that the student didn't complete that makes the difference between the grade the student has selected and the grade that best reflects their work. Why not give students every opportunity to learn more?

* Invite the student to revise the semester letter if it's not a detailed enough story to support the grade selected.

* Add details a student has omitted from a story and explain why a *higher* grade best captures their work.

In the end, after whatever conversation we need to have, I usually let the student make the final call. In the years since I gave up points as the path to final grades in my class, I can count on one hand the number of students I've had to have extended negotiations with. Truly, students can do a great job at selecting their own final grades.

Focusing on progress and growth over mastery for students' grades shifts their focus onto what it takes to actually read and write and do these things well. There is a stronger emphasis on completing work for the grade, but this is not grading for completion or grading for compliance. It is anything but, and I'm OK with using the final grade to emphasize the *doing of the work* more than the *achieving of the standards*. Students who have been collecting points for years may not be learning very much, and they need a massive intervention to stop behaviors that earn points but don't lead to learning.

Our classrooms are only one piece of a huge system that also includes any school-, district-, or state-mandated assessments and testing. These assessments produce the kind of numerical data that some stakeholders need and want so they can make comparisons and track achievement from year to year. I don't need to add to that large body of data. I can focus on what best serves my students day to day in my classroom and give them a safe space to rehearse for those other assessments where they'll be evaluated.

Interlude

Semester Grade Letter by Aracely, Grade 12, Senior Literature, Composition, and Communication

Dear Doc. Z,

I walked to class one day just to see a note on your door: "6th hour meets in the Library Viewing room." I remember being so annoyed at how much I walked down to class, just to walk to the place I had originally come from until I remembered we were getting to choose our choice books. When I arrived at the viewing room, we all sat down around the room and in front of us, there were so many books! Small books, comic books, poetry books, etc. I noticed how thankful I was at this moment to have access to so many books all at the same time. I opened and felt every book that stood out to me; I caressed the book covers to see some books were significantly older, or some which looked like they've never been touched nor acknowledged before.

Aracely tells a separate small story about each of her three chosen goals.

My seventeen language arts colleagues and I share ten classrooms. We each teach in multiple classrooms each year, and they are not the same classrooms from year to year. This makes it difficult for us to cultivate classroom libraries. But we have a beautiful school library with an awesome librarian who constantly updates our library collection.

"Hey, Aracely have you read this book before? I think you might like it if you haven't, take a look," you said. When you handed me the book I was already very captivated just by simply looking at the complexity of the cover.

"*The Poet X?* Let me take a look!" I said. I had to read simply the first few pages to realize how much the detail Elizabeth Acevedo the author had put into this book. I checked out the book that same day and finished it within a week. You, Doc. Z changed my entire perspective on literature when you handed me *The Poet X,* I found myself shedding tears as I read this book because I saw so much of my life within it that I realized the power stories have. I have achieved reading many books since then and I do believe that I have continued reading beyond the classroom and genuinely enjoying the time it takes me to read.

Aracely substitutes journal for writer's notebook, and I'm fine with that. As you'll see, her writer's notebook became very personal for her, and the word journal certainly reflects that.

A journal is just a journal until you make it YOUR journal! I used to think that it isn't important to personalize the place where you keep your work, but it turns out it's the complete opposite. I bought myself some cute pens from a Korean website that had so many adorable school supplies and they instantly caught my attention. Ever since I bought my pens I started to organize my journal for your class and put effort into its appearance because this journal here is where the magic happens . . . the thinking, that's magical. I think ever since I changed my journal's appearance I was able to do more writing and reflecting because I had this desire to fill every space available until I could no longer find a place to write. I think adding our touch to simple things like a journal can bring so much meaning to it, if we think of it from a journal's perspective; we are its savior and its home. We gave it life by writing that first word, by allowing the pen on the fine sheet of paper, that's when it comes to life. I am now in love with journaling and using cool colorful pens to neatly add my touch to things.

Ever since I can remember I've been given my education basically for free. I failed to realize that what I have here is not given to so many people around the world. I remember I used to say useless things like: "Why am I here taking this class that I won't need in the future?" It was always a complaint until I realized how precious it was to be able to learn and take risks for my education all in one place. I used to be a very shy person and was never a good partner, but this class changed me in a way that made me become a good peer to my classmates. Being shy was never going to get me anywhere in life unless I spoke up . . . unless I took a risk and got out of my comfort zone. Taking risks for the benefit of my education and long term community/communication skills has been life-changing because how was I going to survive anywhere else if I didn't take action and realize what my future needed? The only true answer is taking risks. We all fear something, whether it's socializing, or embarrassing ourselves. We all have to reveal ourselves to the world in order to move ahead with life and although it's a huge risk to take we'll all have to do it in order to learn.

Although this last semester really brought me stress, and hardships . . . it also brought experience, knowledge, and adventure to my life. Growing up is all about learning that not everything will be beautiful and easy but that we must try and see the beauty within even those things. I believe I have grown into being a positive member of society. You opened my eyes to see who I really am. I am a person who cares so much, I care tremendously for the happiness of others and for our existence on this planet. This semester I learned that I am someone who will have an influence on people in the future. No matter how long it takes me to achieve saving our planet I can assure you that I will go to the ends of the world to prove my point to the people and encourage them to take action. I am someone who deserves an A this semester.

Sincerely,
Aracely

Aracely selected an A, and I agreed. Her work absolutely showed the growth she articulated in this letter. In the last paragraph, she hints at her semester project, a powerful piece of art about the trash in our oceans. Aracely was timid and shy when I met her, but she left my class realizing that she has a voice and that her voice has power. This is my dearest hope for all of my students.

Afterword

Point-Less from Day One

"FIND YOUR SEAT ON THE SEATING CHART AND READ THIS SHORT text—put your thoughts in the margins."

By the time the bell rings, my students are all in their seats and reading a one-page text, excerpts I've pulled from Alfie Kohn's "The Case Against Grades" (2011).

I whisper, "Welcome to class. I'm Dr. Zerwin. Keep reading and writing your thoughts in the margins. I'll be with you in a few minutes."

For a solid 10 minutes, my new students read and scribble margin notes.

And then I break the silence.

"Thank you for coming into class, finding your seat, and reading what I asked you to read. We'll hear what you thought in a bit, but first, let's figure out who we are."

I introduce myself briefly and then distribute blank name tents and markers.

"Please write on your name tent the name you wish us to call you—write it big and clear so people can see it across the room. You'll be introducing yourself to the class shortly. While you work on your name tents, talk with the people sitting around you. Introduce yourself and tell them what you thought of the text I had you read today."

Little do my students know that this is the first turn-and-talk opportunity they'll have with a response group, the two or three other people they are sitting with already. Once they appear to be finished with their name tents, we go around the room for students to introduce themselves and give us seven words that capture their response to the excerpts from Kohn's argument about grades.

Now that they've heard a bit about what everyone's thinking, they're primed for a Socratic Seminar.

"What? On the first day of school?" Their faces say this if their voices don't.

"Yes, I'm asking you to work on the first day of school."

I quickly go over my Socratic Seminar guidelines, which invite students to choose to sit in the inner circle and take part in the conversation or to sit in the outer circle and listen.

"Please pull your desk into the middle of the room if you would like to speak in our first Socratic Seminar conversation." And with that, I sit in a student desk and pull it into the middle and *hope* that at least a few brave students will join me.

It's a risky play for the first day of school.

Thankfully, I've never been left out there alone. In some classes most students want in the circle. In others, there's a handful, but enough students to sustain conversation. It's a short seminar. It's the first day of school after all. But the text with its radical take on grades makes them want to talk.

I throw out my opening question: "Is Alfie Kohn right about grades or is his argument total crap?"

I go silent. They talk. I listen. I take notes. I start getting to know the humans I've met just 20 minutes before. But I keep an eye on the clock—I need the last few minutes for one last important task.

Invariably, a student will ask me, "So will we have grades in this class or not?"

It's a perfect segue for me to tell them about their first assignment. My syllabus is in the form of a letter (See Online Resources 4.1 and 4.2 for examples). Students read it and write back to tell me what I need to know about each of them as a reader, writer, and human being to be their teacher.

My seminars always end with a critique so we can hear from the outside circle. "What did you notice about this seminar conversation today?" We take a few minutes to hear feedback on our very first seminar conversation together.

My last task is an exit ticket: What questions do you have about this class? I am aware that I've told them nothing about what we'll study in the class, so I want to see what they are wondering about. I'll read over their exit tickets and open our next class together with responses to the questions they pose that my letter/syllabus does not answer.

I thank them for coming to class and tell them how excited I am to spend the year reading and writing with them. And off they go.

This opening day plan is absolutely critical. I crafted it very carefully to seed the kind of classroom experience I intend for my students. We start with reading something, annotating it, and discussing it based on what *they* think about it. This shows them that we will work together at reading and that the focus will be on their meaning making, not mine. Each student's voice surfaces in class on the first day at least twice: when they introduce themselves and offer their seven-word response to the text and when they participate in the seminar. Those who don't choose to pull their desks into the conversation will still have to say something in the critique at the end of the conversation. They won't be able to hide in the class—their voices and thoughts will be necessary. They will also do some writing on the very first day that

FOURTEEN FIRST STEPS
YOU CAN TAKE TO GO POINT-LESS

1. Talk about grades and points less frequently. Avoid talking about them on the first day of school, at back-to-school night with parents, and in parent-teacher conferences. Talk instead about the meaningful work students will do or have done.

2. Teach students to reflect on their learning. (Chapter 6)

3. Do more grading based on simply whether or not students completed the task. You do not have to evaluate everything. (Chapter 5)

4. Take the numbers off of the rubric. (Chapter 4)

5. Ask students to write narratives about their work based on the rubric and collect the narratives instead of marking scores on the rubric. (Chapter 4)

6. Turn a points-based rubric into a checklist of the characteristics of high-quality work and use that as feedback instead of evaluation. (Chapter 4)

7. Choose *one* category in your grade book and think about how you could manage it without points. (Chapter 5)

8. Hold off on assigning grades to a task until as late as possible.

9. Type something besides a number in the score box in your grade book just to see if you can. (Chapter 5)

10. Ask your administration if you can have more flexibility with your grade book. (Chapter 5)

11. Have more conferences with students. (Chapter 4)

12. Do grades as usual, but at semester's end, ask students how well the number in the grade book captures what they learned, and have them write to you about it.

13. Have an open, honest conversation with your students about grades.

14. Just try something and see what happens.

has an authentic purpose. I need their exit ticket words to prepare my plan for the next day when I'll respond to their questions about the class.

And the centerpiece of the class period is a discussion about why grades don't support learners. From day one, we engage the conversation. This gets my students thinking immediately about what it might mean to focus on learning instead of point collecting.

With one 50-minute class, I've shown students that they should expect to read, to have thoughts about the reading, to discuss those thoughts, and to write for real purposes. I have already started their work toward the learning goals for the course.

Also, they should expect that grades will be different from what they might be used to. Because we've only had time to barely start the conversation about grades and learning, I hope they will be sufficiently curious to come back the next day with some healthy anticipation.

Expect That Students Want to Learn

When we ask our students to do something different without explaining to them how what they're used to doesn't serve them well as learners, they will push back. I learned this the hard way. But when we engage students in real conversation about how well school has supported their growth as learners and *listen* to what they have to say, they start to trust that we're on their side. They see that we value their experiences in school. They see that we care about their dreams and goals for their lives. They see that we want to make our classrooms a space where they will do work that matters to them. They start to believe that we are really, truly, stepping outside of the game of school as they know it, and they will come with us.

The truth is that high school students want to read and want to write, as long as that work matters to who they are as human beings. Penny Kittle says in *Book Love* (2012) that "teenagers want to read, if we let them." We just have to get out of their way. And we need to take our traditional notions about grading with us. Strict rubrics. Unyielding point systems. Late work penalties. Grading scales. Grade books that broadcast up-to-the-minute percentage-based grades with high stakes attached.

We built all of this—because we thought that students wouldn't work without these things? It doesn't really matter why we built it—we can also take it down. The point-less approach has saved me some time in responding to my students' work. And the time I'm spending is more productive and meaningful—for me and for my students. I'm energized by responding as a reader rather than an evaluator. I love being a part of the reading/writing community my classroom has become. The work I'm doing helps my students grow as readers and writers—it's not all just the exhausting red pen efforts that the grading system seemed to ask of me. The work I do is qualitatively different now, I see readers and writers acting with more agency in my classroom, and I feel more agency as their teacher too.

I believe your students will follow you away from a classroom experience that rewards them with points for their compliance *if* they can see clearly that the place they're headed is worth it. Show them that it is.

It's scary for them, too. Students have become comfortable with the system we've created. They are used to working for points. They may need some help stepping away from that.

But trust that students can go with you. Trust that they want to.

And trust that you can lead them there.

More	Less
Feedback	Grades and points
Student reflection	Teacher evaluation
Students knowing what they know and need to learn	Students waiting for the numbers in the grade book to tell them what they know
Students doing reading and writing	Students faking reading and only writing to satisfy a rubric
Student-centered	Teacher-centered
Emphasis on process and revision	Emphasis on perfect, polished final products for a grade
Students talking to each other about their work	Students competing with each other for points
Authentic audiences and purposes for student work	Teacher-only audience for student work; teacher evaluation only purpose for student work
Students getting feedback from each other	Teacher-only feedback giver
Transparency about what it takes to learn	Transparency about what it takes to earn points
Teacher mentoring/modeling/coaching	Teacher giving inflexible mandates backed up by points
Conferences	Written feedback on everything
Focused, clear, easy to remember learning goals	Extensive lists of required standards
Inviting students to work for reasons meaningful for them	Forcing students to work for points
Emphasis on students doing authentic work	Emphasis on students mastering skills or collecting knowledge
Qualitative data in grade book	Quantitative data in grade book

A.1 "More and Less" Chart

Bibliography

Baca, Jimmy Santiago. 2001. *A Place to Stand*. New York: Grove.

Bower, Joe. *For the Love of Learning* (blog). http://joebower.blogspot.com/.

Bower, Joe, and P. L. Thomas, eds. 2013. *De-Testing + De-Grading Schools: Authentic Alternatives to Accountability and Standardization*. New York: Peter Lang.

Carr, Nicolas. 2011. *The Shallows*. New York: W.W. Norton.

Chiaravalli, Arthur. 2017. "Teachers Going Gradeless: Toward a Future of Growth, Not Grades." https://medium.com/teachers-going-gradeless/teachers -going-gradeless-50d621c14cad.

Donovan, Sarah. 2015. "Three Perspectives Improve Peer-to-Peer Response." MiddleWeb. https://www.middleweb.com/24247/3-perspectives -can-improve-peer-to-peer-response/.

Dueck, Myron. 2014. *Grading Smarter Not Harder: Assessment Strategies That Motivate Kids and Help Them Learn*. Alexandria, VA: Association for Supervision and Curriculum Development.

Edmundson, Mark. 2002. *Teacher: The One Who Made the Difference*. New York: Random House.

Emerson, Ralph Waldo. 1837. "The American Scholar." *Digital Emerson: A Collective Archive*. http://digitalemerson.wsulibs.wsu.edu/exhibits/show/text /the-american-scholar.

Ferriter, William, and Paul Cancellieri. 2017. *Creating a Culture of Feedback*. Bloomington, IN: Solution Tree Press.

Fletcher, Ralph. 1993. *What a Writer Needs*. Portsmouth, NH: Heinemann.

Gallagher, Kelly. 2009. *Readicide: How Schools Are Killing Reading and What You Can Do About It*. Portland, ME: Stenhouse.

———. 2011. *Write Like This: Teaching Real-World Writing Through Modeling and Mentor Texts*. Portland, ME: Stenhouse.

———. 2015. *In the Best Interest of Students: Staying True to What Works in the ELA Classroom.* Portland, ME: Stenhouse.

Gallagher, Kelly, and Penny Kittle. 2018. *180 Days: Two Teachers and the Quest to Engage and Empower Adolescents.* Portsmouth, NH: Heinemann.

Guskey, Thomas. 2015. *On Your Mark: Challenging the Conventions of Grading and Reporting.* Bloomington, IN: Solution Tree Press.

Guskey, Thomas, and Jane Bailey. 2001. *Developing Grading and Reporting Systems for Student Learning.* Thousand Oaks, CA: Corwin.

Hattie, John. 2008. *Visible Learning: A Synthesis of Over 800 Meta-Analyses Relating to Achievement.* New York: Routledge.

Inoue, Asao B. 2015. *Antiracist Writing Assessment Ecologies: Teaching and Assessing Writing for a Socially Just Future.* Fort Collins, CO: WAC Clearinghouse; Anderson, SC: Parlor Press.

Kesey, Ken. 1962. *One Flew Over the Cuckoo's Nest.* New York: Signet.

Kittle, Penny. 2008. *Write Beside Them: Risk, Voice, and Clarity in High School Writing.* Portsmouth, NH: Heinemann.

———. 2012. *Book Love: Developing Depth, Stamina, and Passion in Adolescent Readers.* Portsmouth, NH: Heinemann.

Kohn, Alfie. 2011. "The Case Against Grades." https://www.alfiekohn.org/article/case-grades/.

Krakauer, Jon. 1996. *Into the Wild.* New York: Anchor Books.

Lane, Barry. 1993. *After The End: Teaching and Learning Creative Revision.* Portsmouth, NH: Heinemann.

Marchetti, Allison, and Rebekah O'Dell. 2015. *Writing with Mentors: How to Reach Every Writer in the Room Using Current, Engaging Mentor Texts.* Portsmouth, NH: Heinemann.

Marzano, Robert J. 2000. *Transforming Classroom Grading.* Alexandria, VA: Association for Supervision and Curriculum Development.

McTighe, Jay. 2012. "Designing an Understanding-Based Curriculum Around Common Core Standards." https://dpi.wi.gov/sites/default/files/imce/ela/resources/McTighe_Handout_1%5B1%5D.pdf.

Minor, Cornelius. 2017. "Staring Down Dragons: The Terrifying Nature of Possibility." Luncheon address at the Conference on English Leadership National Convention, St. Louis, MO, November.

Morrison, Toni. 1987. *Beloved*. New York: Alfred A. Knopf.

National Governors Association Center for Best Practices and Council of Chief State School Officers. 2010. Common Core State Standards. Washington, DC: NGA and CCSSO. www.corestandards.org/.

Newkirk, Thomas. 2014. *Minds Made for Stories: How We Really Read and Write Information and Persuasive Texts*. Portsmouth, NH: Heinemann.

Newport, Cal. 2016. *Deep Work: Rules for Focused Success in a Distracted World*. New York: Grand Central.

Nilson, Linda. 2013. *Creating Self-Regulated Learners: Strategies to Strengthen Students' Self-Awareness and Learning Skills*. Sterling, VA: Stylus.

Pellegrino, James, Naomi Chudowsky, and Robert Glaser, eds. 2001. "Executive Summary: Knowing What Students Know: The Science and Design of Educational Assessment." National Research Council. https://www.nap.edu /read/10019/chapter/2.

Prather, Liz. 2017. *Project-Based Writing: Teaching Writers to Manage Time and Clarify Purpose*. Portsmouth, NH: Heinemann.

Quate, Stevie. 2019. "Writer's Notebook." *Writing Workshop Basics*. https://sites .google.com/view/basics-writingworkshop/writers-notebook.

Ray, Katie Wood. 2001. *The Writing Workshop: Working Through the Hard Parts (And They're All Hard Parts)*. Urbana, IL: National Council of Teachers of English.

Rief, Linda. 2014. *Read, Write, Teach: Choice and Challenge in the Reading–Writing Workshop*. Portsmouth, NH: Heinemann.

Romano, Tom. 2013. *Fearless Writing: Multigenre to Motivate and Inspire*. Portsmouth, NH: Heinemann.

Schimmer, Tom. 2016. *Grading from the Inside Out: Bringing Accuracy to Student Assessment Through a Standards-Based Mindset*. Bloomington, IN: Solution Tree Press.

Shepard, Lorrie, Phil Daro, and Fran Stancavage. 2013. "The Relevance of Learning Progressions for NAEP." Commissioned by the NAEP Validity Studies Panel. https://files.eric.ed.gov/fulltext/ED545240.pdf.

Stiggins, Rick. 2017. *The Perfect Assessment System*. Alexandria, VA: Association for Supervision and Curriculum Development.

Teachers Going Gradeless (blog). https://teachersgoinggradeless.com/.

Thomas, Paul. *Radical Eyes for Equity* (blog). https://radicalscholarship.wordpress.com/.

Torres, Julia. 2018. "Going Gradeless in Urban Ed." *Teachers Going Gradeless* (blog). www.teachersgoinggradeless.com/blog/2018/03/10/urban-ed.

Tyack, David. 1974. *The One Best System: A History of American Urban Education*. Cambridge, MA: Harvard University Press.

Visible Learning. 2017. "Hattie Ranking: 252 Influences and Effect Sizes Related to Student Achievement." https://visible-learning.org/hattie-ranking-influences -effect-sizes-learning-achievement/.

Vonnegut, Kurt. 1969. *Slaughterhouse Five*. New York: Dial Press.

Willis, Paul. 1977. *Learning to Labor: How Working Class Kids Get Working Class Jobs*. Westmead, UK: Saxon House.

Wilson, Maja. 2006. *Rethinking Rubrics in Writing Assessment*. Portsmouth, NH: Heinemann.

———. 2018. *Reimagining Writing Assessment: From Scales to Stories*. Portsmouth, NH: Heinemann.

Wirth, Karl, and Dexter Perkins. 2008. "Learning to Learn." http://www.montana .edu/rmaher/barrier_courses/Learning%20to%20Learn%20Wirth.pdf.

Wormeli, Rick. 2006. *Fair Isn't Always Equal: Assessing and Grading in the Dif- ferentiated Classroom*. Portland, ME: Stenhouse.